New Jersey

WILDLIFE VIEWING GUIDE

Written and edited by
Laurie Pettigrew
Sharon Mallman

Adventure Publications, Inc.
Cambridge, Minnesota

ACKNOWLEDGEMENTS

The New Jersey Department of Environmental Protection's Division of Fish and Wildlife wish to thank the Wildlife Viewing Guide Steering Committee for providing direction and insight, contributing ideas and si▮ nominations, and offering peer review and editorial comment during this project.

Steering Committee

Laurie Pettigrew, NJDEP Division of Fish and Wildlife

Lillian Armstrong, New Jersey Audubon Society

Steve Eisenhauer, Natural Lands Trust

Karen Hatcher, Celebrate New Jersey

Diane Hewlett-Lowrie, NJDEP Division of Parks and Forestry

Brian Johnson, Natural Lands Trust

Bruce Lane, National Park Service

Jim Mallman, Watchable Wildlife, Inc.

Tony McBride, NJDEP Division of Fish and Wildlife

Margaret O'Gorman, Conserve Wildlife Foundation of New Jersey

Terry O'Leary, Forest Resource Education Center

Phyllis Oppenheimer, Department of State, Division of Travel and Tourism

Jim Sciascia, NJDEP Division of Fish and Wildlife

Arthur Webster, United States Fish and Wildlife Service

Special Thanks

The Division of Fish and Wildlife also wishes to thank all those whose special knowledge of the state's natura▮ areas contributed to the guide—individuals from county parks and recreation departments, conservation org▮ nizations, wildlife biologists, park rangers, foresters, birdwatchers and others too numerous to name. Special thanks go to Lillian Armstrong, Emile DeVito, Mim Dunne, Diane Hewlett-Lowrie, Karen Johnson, Sharon Mallman and Barbara Steele for providing their experience and expertise. In addition, all of the photographic art used to beautifully illustrate this guide was very generously donated by the featured photographers.

Book and cover design by Jonathan Norberg (all rights reserved)

Photo Credits: (all photos copyrighted by their respective photographers, with all rights reserved)
Front cover photos: red knot by Bruce Taubert, Cope's gray treefrog by Stan Tekiela, monarch butterfly ▮ John Parke

Back cover photos: wildflower field, painted turtle and red squirrel by Jim Mallman, greater yellowlegs by Bob Cunningham, black swallowtail butterfly by John Parke

Lillian Armstrong/NJAS: 15 (bottom) **Steve Byland:** 17 (white-breasted nuthatch), 47 (northern harrier) 131 (brown pelican), 161 (house wren) 189 (blue dasher) **Kathy Clark:** 11 (peregrine falcon)
Bob Cunningham: 105 (orchard oriole), 130-133 (Forsythe National Wildlife Refuge), 205 (laughing gull)
Jim Mallman: 10 (beaver), 21 (bald eagle) **John Parke:** 11, 20-23 (Musconetong Valley), 46-49 (Round Valley Reservoir) **Mark Peck:** 10 (red knot) **Laurie Pettigrew/NJDFW:** 14, 15 (top), 16, 104-107 (Assunpink Wildlife Management Area), 160-163 (Greenwood Forest Wildlife Management Area), 188-189 (Abbotts Meadow Wildlife Management Area), 204-207 (Dix Wildlife Management Area)
Gina Provenzano/NJDPF: 82-83 (Liberty State Park) **Kim Steininger:** 83 (peregrine falcon)

10 9 8 7 6 5 4 3 2 1

New Jersey Wildlife Viewing Guide
Copyright 2009 by Watchable Wildlife, Inc.
Published by Adventure Publications, Inc.
820 Cleveland St. S
Cambridge, MN 55008
1-800-678-7006
www.adventurepublications.net
Printed in China
ISBN-13: 978-1-59193-240-6
ISBN-10: 1-59193-240-8

"TO HELP COMMUNITIES AND WILDLIFE PROSPER"

A simple mission statement for a complex challenge; Watchable Wildlife, Inc. is an independent nonprofit working with communities across North America, promoting a better understanding of the real value of their wildlife and remaining wild places.

Partnering with state and federal wildlife agencies, we assist, when asked, in developing sustainable and economically viable wildlife/nature tourism programs. We work towards accomplishing this mission of developing sustainable wildlife-viewing programs by focusing on three key areas: our annual conference, publications like this viewing guide and on-the-ground projects.

Our annual Watchable Wildlife Conference is the industry's best vehicle for presenting new ideas. It also serves as an international forum for training and recognizing the works of professionals in the field of wildlife viewing. Watchable Wildlife, Inc. works hands-on with conservation-minded partners on projects across the continent to develop safe, satisfying and sustainable wildlife viewing.

Our Viewing Guide series is a continent-wide effort to meet the needs of North America's growing wildlife-viewing public. The guides encourage people to observe wildlife in natural settings and provide them with information on where and when to go and what to expect when they get there. We believe the presence of wildlife-viewing sites near communities has positive social and economic impacts.

We want wildlife viewing to be fun. However we also believe it should be an economically viable resource for the host community. In the larger context, we want people to learn about wildlife, to care about it and to conserve it.

For more information about Watchable Wildlife, Inc., this year's conference, our other publications and our current projects, visit www.watchablewildlife.org.

Yours truly,

James Mallman
President, Watchable Wildlife, Inc.
www.watchablewildlife.org

Brown road signs with the binoculars logo let travelers know that they're in a great spot to see some wildlife! These uniform signs are officially approved by the U.S. Department of Transportation and are one example of the programs sponsored by Watchable Wildlife, Inc.

Table of Contents

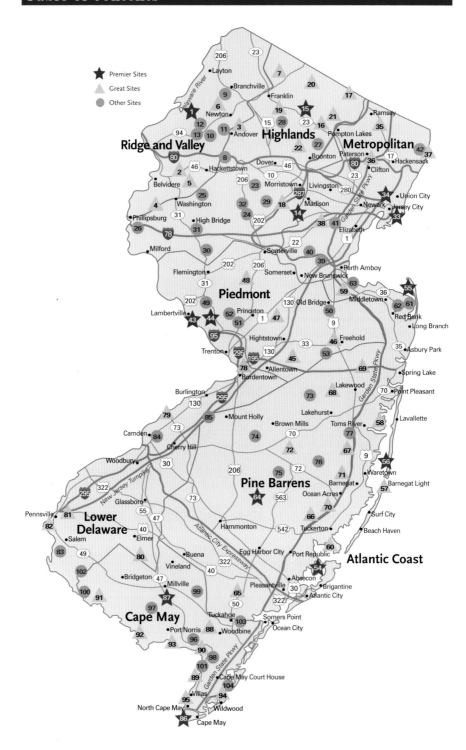

Premier Sites
Great Sites
Other Sites

Delaware River

206
23
•Layton
7
20
•Branchville
17
•Franklin
9
19
•Ramsey
6
15
•Newton
Highlands
Metropolitan
12
15 28 23 16
21
35
94 13 10 11 3 •Andover
22 27
Pompton Lakes
42 37
Ridge and Valley
8
Dover• 46
Boonton• Paterson•
17
80
46 •Hackettstown
80 36 •Hackensack
2
206
10
Clifton
Belvidere• 5
23 •Morristown•
Livingston• 23
25
287
280
34 •Union City
4
Washington
32 29 18
Madison•
Newark• Jersey City
31
24
14
38 41
33
•Phillipsburg
•High Bridge
202
Elizabeth
26
78
22
1
31
Milford•
30
•Somerville
40
202
206
39
•Perth Amboy
Flemington•
Somerset• New Brunswick•
59
63 36 55
31
48
Piedmont
50
62 61
202
49
130 Old Bridge•
Middletown•
•Red Bank
Lambertville•
52 Princeton•
1 47
9
•Long Branch
43 44 51
95
Hightstown•
33 46
Freehold•
35 •Asbury Park
Trenton• 295
130
45 53
78
•Allentown
69
•Spring Lake
195
•Bordentown
Lakewood•
70 •Point Pleasant
Burlington•
73 68
295
130
79
85 •Mount Holly
Lakehurst•
•Lavallette
73
•Brown Mills
Toms River• 58
Camden•
84
74
70
77
Cherry Hill•
72
67 9
Woodbury•
30
76
56
206
75 72
71 •Waretown
322
Pine Barrens
Barnegat• Barnegat Light
Glassboro•
64 563
Ocean Acres• 57
295
73
70
Pennsville• 81
55
66 •Surf City
Lower
47
Hammonton•
542 Tuckerton•
82
Delaware
40
•Beach Haven
•Salem
•Elmer
60
83 49
80
•Buena
Egg Harbor City •Port Republic
Atlantic Coast
102
Vineland•
40 322
•Absecon
100 91
•Bridgeton 47 •Millville
99
Pleasantville• 30 •Brigantine
97
65
•Atlantic City
87
50 322•
Cape May
Tuckahoe•
103 Somers Point•
92
88 •Woodbine
•Ocean City
93 96
90
98
101
89 •Cape May Court House
104
•Villas 94
95
North Cape May• •Wildwood
86 •Cape May

4

Table of Contents

Number indication on map: Premier Sites Great Sites Other Sites

Number indication on map: ★ Premier Sites ▲ Great Sites ● Other Sites

Number indication on map: Premier Sites   Great Sites ● Other Sites   **7**

Number indication on map: Premier Sites   Great Sites   ● Other Sites   **9**

Wildlife Worth Celebrating

New Jersey is home to approximately 535 species of vertebrate wildlife, including 85 species of freshwater fish, and the coastline supports 28 marine mammals and 336 species of marine fish. This incredible diversity of wildlife in such a small state can be attributed to both geographic position and geologic history. New Jersey lies firmly within the Atlantic Flyway—the easternmost migratory pathway in North America. Many southern species reach their northernmost range here, while many northern species reach their southernmost range. In addition, seven distinct physiographic regions provide a diversity of habitats that support abundant wildlife.

Go to www.njfishandwildlife.com/chklists.htm to download checklists of New Jersey wildlife.

Red Knot

Shorebirds

The Delaware Estuary is the site of one of the natural world's most amazing phenomenons—the coincidence of spawning horseshoe crabs and the northward migration of shorebirds. The shores of Delaware Bay provide essential spawning habitat for the world's largest concentration of horseshoe crabs and critical stopover habitat for millions of shorebirds that arrive each spring to feast on crab eggs. The bayshore beaches and adjacent salt marshes teem with shorebirds from early May to mid-June. The protein-rich crab eggs fuel the incredible journey of the shorebirds to their breeding ground in the Arctic. The birds arrive thin and hungry from their nonstop flight from South America and need to double their weight quickly before leaving on the long flight north.

Shorebird species are easily disturbed by people walking and by pets playing on beaches. If birds are disturbed while resting or feeding, they may not build up the necessary fat reserves to make it to their Arctic breeding grounds. You can help by observing a few simple rules:

⬩ Observe beach closures on posted beaches.

⬩ Use designated viewing areas—do not walk on the beach when the shorebirds are present.

⬩ Study shorebirds from a distance with binoculars or a scope.

Beaver

Mammals

New Jersey boasts 64 terrestrial mammals and 28 marine mammals. From black bears and pygmy shrews to little brown bats, woodchuck and river otters to humpback whales, New Jersey's mammals are small and large, can run, climb, swim, or fly, live in water or on land. With such a wealth of warm-blooded creatures, you might expect that mammals are easy to spot. Unfortunately, it is often difficult to see mammals unless you understand their behavior. Learning about a mammal's habits and habitat will make it easier to find. Reading and identifying wildlife signs like scat and tracks will provide clues to the presence of these elusive and fascinating animals.

Timber Rattlesnake

Reptiles and Amphibians

When it comes to "herping," (searching for amphibians and reptiles), New Jersey holds its own. The state officially lists 72 species of reptiles and amphibians, but the herp enthusiast can consistently find 36 species statewide. New Jersey may not rival the sheer number of species found in places like Virginia, but its unique geology means we have species that can be seen as far south as Florida, as far north as Canada, or as far west as Texas.

Success Stories

In the 1800s, the osprey was common along New Jersey's coastlines. By the mid-1970s however, this fish-eating raptor had declined to only 53 pairs due to habitat loss and the use of the pesticide DDT. In 1979, the NJDEP's Division of Fish and Wildlife Endangered and Nongame Species Program began a reintroduction program. Gradually the population began to recover. By 2001 there were over 300 pairs statewide. Look for these magnificent birds along both coasts and over many large inland bodies of water from March through October.

Peregrine falcons traditionally nested on the cliffs of the Palisades and rocky outcroppings in the Highlands. However, by 1960, there were no known pairs of peregrines east of the Mississippi due to the use of DDT. The birds were listed on the federal and state endangered species lists in the 1970s and in 1975, a national peregrine recovery plan was put into action. Today, New Jersey has 15 pairs of peregrines statewide.

Peregrine Falcon

Biologists from NJDEP's Division of Fish and Wildlife Endangered and Nongame Species Program began a bold and successful bald eagle recovery project in 1982. There was a single bald eagle nest in 1982; in 2008, there were over 60. Today, bald eagles can be seen all along the Delaware Bayshore and the lower Delaware River and on many of the larger bodies of water in the northern part of the state.

The wild turkey disappeared from New Jersey by the mid-1800s due to changes in land use and over-harvesting for food. The NJDEP's Division of Fish and Wildlife teamed up with the NJ Chapter of the National Wild Turkey Federation to reintroduce turkeys to the state in 1977. The population is now estimated to be around 20,000 statewide. Wild turkeys can be seen at any time of the year throughout the state.

Read about reintroduction programs and success stories at www.njfishandwildlife.com.

Places to Go

New Jersey is home to many kinds of wildlife, from its 127-mile coastline with shorebirds and marine mammals to its fields and forests teeming with grassland and forest-dwelling birds and animals. The many places described in this book comprise the best of the best, a sampling of all that New Jersey offers to the wildlife watcher. In this book, the reader will find:

National Parks, Monuments and Recreation Areas

The National Park Service, U.S. Department of the Interior manages 11 national parks, historic sites, monuments and recreation areas in New Jersey. These include the country's first national reserve, the New Jersey Pinelands National Reserve, which includes portions of seven southern New Jersey counties and encompasses over one million acres of farms, forests and wetlands.

Wildlife Refuges

The U.S. Fish and Wildlife Service, also within the Department of the Interior, manages five national wildlife refuges in New Jersey. They offer outstanding wildlife viewing in most of the physiographic regions of the state, from coastal birds to migrating songbirds, raptors and large upland mammals.

State Parks, Forests and Historic Sites

The New Jersey Department of Environmental Protection, Division of Parks and Forestry manages 39 state parks, 11 state forests, three recreation areas, 42 natural areas, five state marinas and 57 historic sites, many of which are featured in this guide. From New Jersey's highest point at High Point State Park to its lowest at Cape May Point State Park, the preservation and stewardship of the state's diverse natural, recreational and historic resources is the central mission of the Division of Parks and Forestry. Explore forests and beaches, paddle a tidal creek or swift-running river, hike a rugged mountain trail or meander along a sand road in Wharton State Forest. It's all possible at one of New Jersey's fabulous state attractions.

Wildlife Management Areas

The New Jersey Department of Environmental Protection, Division of Fish and Wildlife manages more than 324,000 acres in 122 Wildlife Management Areas (WMA). Thousands of migrating warblers, raptors and shorebirds stop to rest and feed at Higbee Beach WMA in spring and fall, making it one of the nation's premier bird watching spots. Some of the state's best warm-water fishing can be found on WMAs such as Union Lake, Assunpink and Menantico—where the state record largemouth bass was caught. If you prefer, spend a day hiking over rugged terrain looking for white-tailed deer, black bear and porcupine at Sparta Mountain or Berkshire Valley.

✕ NJ Audubon Society Birding and Wildlife Trails

The Birding and Wildlife Trails (BWT) create numerous local loops of "trails" utilizing the existing transportation infrastructure to bring visitors to wildlife-watching locations. The BWT Project encourages community participation, ownership and support of the BWTs in the pursuit of nature tourism. As of this printing, over 200 wildlife-viewing sites have been included in two dozen driving routes along the Delaware Bayshore, the Hackensack River and in the northwestern Skylands region. More trails are being developed each year with plans to cover the whole state over the next several years. Visit www.njwildlifetrails.org for detailed information on New Jersey's Birding and Wildlife Trails and links to help you plan your trip as well.

New Jersey's Green Acres Program

New Jersey is a small, densely populated state with a high percentage of public open space. Much of this is due to the success of the Green Acres Program, created in 1961 to meet the state's growing recreation and conservation needs. Together with public and private partners, Green Acres has protected almost 640,000 acres of open space and provided hundreds of outdoor recreational facilities in communities around the state.

As residents of the most densely populated state in the nation, New Jerseyans have long supported open-space preservation. This commitment is demonstrated through the approval of 12 statewide Green Acres ballot initiatives since 1961. These initiatives have generated a $3 billion investment in protecting unique landscapes and natural resources, providing quality recreational opportunities and preserving heritage at historic sites across the state. The state has partnered with local government in acquiring lands that protect critical water supplies and habitat for a wide range of special plants and animals. These programs also maintain the "Garden" in the Garden State by preserving farmland and safeguarding our unique and irreplaceable landscapes and historic sites.

Important Bird Areas

The National Audubon Society, in partnership with BirdLife International, is identifying a network of sites in the United States that provide critical habitat for birds. This global effort, known as the Important Bird Areas Program (IBA), has been initiated in all 50 states. More than 1,900 state-level IBAs encompassing over 140 million acres have been identified, with a goal of 3,000 designated IBAs around the world. The IBA Program sets science-based priorities for habitat conservation and promotes positive action to safeguard vital bird habitats. New Jersey's IBA program was developed by NJAS and designates both important bird and birding areas (IBBA). Go to www.njaudubon.org to learn more about New Jersey's 149 IBBAs and IBBA program.

Wildlife are Watching

We've all had it happen. You look up from the trail just in time to see an animal dive out of sight—a swoop of wing, a flash of antler, a slap of a beaver's tail. The problem is that many of us just do not understand some of the simple tips for watching wildlife. Take a few minutes to review these pointers and share them with others and watch wildlife like the pros.

The truth is, most animals see, hear and smell us long before we catch their drift. They size us up, and depending on how far away we are and how we act, they decide whether to stay, defend themselves or flee. Fighting and fleeing rob them of precious energy.

Fortunately, there are simple ways you can help blend into an animal's surroundings. In return, you'll be treated to a wildlife show that will make your heart pound and your senses hum.

WINNING THE WILDLIFE SWEEPSTAKES

The ultimate wildlife watching experience is behavior watching—viewing animals without interrupting their normal activities. Instead of just a glimpse, you have an encounter—a chance not only to identify the animal, but to identify with it.

Fade into the Woodwork

- Wear natural colors and unscented lotions.

- Remove glasses that glint.

- Walk softly so as not to snap twigs.

- Crouch behind boulders or vegetation to hide your figure or break up your outline.

- Try not to throw a shadow.

- Remember that your reflection may show in a pool of water.

Let Animals Be Themselves

- Resist the temptation to "save" baby animals. Mom is usually watching from a safe distance.

- Let animals eat their natural foods. Sharing your sandwich may harm a wild animal's digestive system and get animals hooked on handouts. Animals fed by humans may eventually lose their fear of cars, campers or even poachers. As a bonus, you'll learn a lot about an animal by watching what food it prefers.

- Let patience reward you. Resist the urge to throw rocks to see a flock fly.

- Savor the experience of being in an animal's home. Absorb all that it can teach you about living gently upon the land.

Stick to the Sidelines

⌃ Use binoculars or zoom lenses to get a close-up. Aim for pictures of assured, dignified animals instead of stressed, panting victims.

⌃ Give nests a wide berth. Although you mean well, your visit may lead a predator to the nest or cause the parents to jump ship, exposing eggs or young to the elements.

Come to Your Senses

⌃ A wildlife encounter is a spectrum of sensations. Deepen awareness by tapping your senses of smell, taste, touch, hearing and sight.

⌃ Focus and expand your attention, taking in the foreground and then switching to take in the wide view.

⌃ Use your peripheral vision rather than turning your head.

⌃ Look for out-of-place shapes—horizontal shapes in a mostly vertical forest or an oblong shape on a tree branch.

⌃ Watch for out-of-place motions—the flight of a bird, for instance, stands out against a backdrop of falling leaves.

⌃ Look above and below you. Animals occupy niches in all the vertical and horizontal layers of a habitat.

⌃ Make "mule ears." Cup your hands around the back of your ears to amplify the natural sounds.

⌃ Heed your instincts. If the hair on the back of your neck stands up (a vestige of the days when we had fur), an animal may be near.

⌃ Silence can speak volumes. Animals may fall silent when a predator is passing through an area.

Be Easy to Be with

⌃ Relax your muscles. Animals can easily detect tension.

⌃ Make yourself as small and unassuming as possible.

⌃ Move like molasses—slow, smooth and steady.

⌃ If you must advance, take a roundabout route. Never move directly toward an animal.

⌃ Avert your gaze; animals may interpret a direct stare as a threat.

Think Like an Animal

⌃ Imagine how the animal you are seeking spends its days. Check field guides to find out about life history and preferred habitats.

⌃ As a rule, the border between two habitats is a good place to see residents from both places.

⌃ Look in high-visitation areas: trails, intersections, perches, ledges overlooking open areas and drinking sites.

⌃ Take note of the season and gauge whether the animal will be seeking a mate, feathering its nest, fattening for the winter or preparing to migrate.

⌃ Figure out the best time of day for viewing by imagining an animal's daily schedule. When does it feed? Nap? Bathe? Drink? Dusk and dawn are usually good bets.

⌃ Factor in the weather. After a rain, for instance, many animals emerge to feed on displaced insects, flooded-out rodents and so on.

IN SUMMARY

If you long to be wrapped up in watching, follow these tips from experienced behavior watchers. With the right combination of patience and know-how, you'll be able to witness wildlife without startling them or sapping their energy. It's a feeling you'll never forget!

Support local businesses and tell them you are here to watch wildlife in their region. It helps encourage local conservation.

CAMERA TIPS

⌃ Use at least a 400 mm lens.

⌃ Position yourself with the sun at your back.

⌃ Afternoon light is best.

⌃ Aim for featuring wildlife with natural surroundings, not a full-frame profile.

How to Use This Guide

The sites featured in this book have been divided into eight regions:
Ridge and Valley
Highlands
Metropolitan
Piedmont
Atlantic Coast
Pine Barrens
Lower Delaware River
Cape May-Delaware Bay

Within each region, the sites are categorized into three types:

These are the most significant sites and are the places you'll want to consider visiting if you have only a limited time. Their site narratives run four to six pages.

These are also important wildlife-viewing sites. In some cases, the types of wildlife species that might be seen are more limited. Their site narratives run two pages.

The "other" sites are worth visiting when time is not a factor. They are often small and have limited parking. Please do not be quick to discount these sites as many are magnets for wildlife. Local site narratives are less than a page long.

As you glance through the pages of this guide, you will notice that each site narrative follows the same format. This should make it easy for you to compare sites and find important information.

The site name is the most common name attributed to the site. Sites are organized by regions (Ridge and Valley, Highlands, Metropolitan, Piedmont, Atlantic Coast, Pine Barrens, Lower Delaware River and Cape May-Delaware Bay) and within each region they are organized by type (Premier, Great, Other).

★ Indicates type of site (Premier) and number on map

▲ Indicates type of site (Great) and number on map

● Indicates type of site (Other) and number on map

Description

Mentions some of the key sights and wildlife experiences at the site.

Wildlife to Watch

Gives specific information about the species you might expect to see, the best seasons for viewing and your chances of seeing them. Some natural history information is also provided.

Trails

Features trail information at the site, including trail length, accessibility and difficulty notes.

Site Notes Gives information about the sites, such as the best times to visit, parking or entry fees, permit information or other specific tips.

Size Indicates approximate size of the site.

Directions Gives driving directions to the site from the nearest town.

Nearest town Indicates the town nearest to the site where visitors may find gas, dining, lodging, etc.

Ownership Indicates who owns or is responsible for managing the site.

Contact Provides the site manager's address and telephone number. Note that not all sites have a local office and telephone number. Whenever possible, a website address is provided.

Features Lists of the types of amenities that are available at the site.

Ridge and Valley

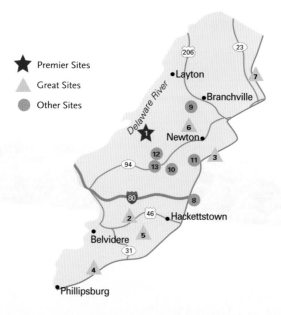

★ Premier Sites

▲ Great Sites

● Other Sites

Layton
Branchville
Newton
Hackettstown
Belvidere
Phillipsburg

Rich in history and wildlife

The Ridge and Valley Region is dominated by the Kittatinny Ridge, which runs northeast to southwest along the Delaware River. The broad valley that lies east of the ridge was carved during the last ice age by a glacier that is estimated to have been a mile thick. The soils of the ridge are typically shallow, rocky and of poor quality, while the valley contains fertile soil and has a long history of agricultural activity.

The Appalachian Trail runs along the crest of the ridge and extends north to Maine and south to Georgia. The Appalachian Trail is accessible from many road crossings and numerous hiking trails.

The ridge itself runs north into New York and south into Pennsylvania. Its vegetation is characteristically oak-hickory and oak-maple forests on its flanks, with pitch pine-scrub oak communities along the summit. There are numerous hemlock ravines along the many brooks that flow off the ridge, although the splendor of these ravines is marred due to a small non-native pest called the woolly adelgid. The area's stands of pine and spruce date back to the New Deal conservation projects of the 1930s. Other notable features include the Delaware Water Gap, at the southern end of the ridge, and High Point State Park in the northwest corner of the state. Sunrise Mountain, in Stokes State Forest, is popular for its vistas and as a gathering place for viewing the annual raptor migration in the fall. The ridge-and-valley topography creates air flow patterns that aid raptors and other birds during migration.

The area is rich in history as well as wildlife. The Old Mine Road, running along the Delaware River from the Water Gap to Port Jervis, New York, is the oldest commercial road in the U.S. and was originally constructed by the Dutch to transport copper from local mines. These mines are visible from the Coppermine Trail in the recreation area. There are also countless old stone "fences" throughout the area, old cemeteries and the historic villages of Walpack, Millbrook and Peter's Valley.

Fortunately, much of the region, including the Kittatinny Ridge, is preserved as public land. The entire region is bordered on the west by the Delaware River, which supports a great diversity of fish and wildlife, including osprey, eagles, beavers, otters and a variety of nesting waterfowl. The forested ridge gives birth to trout streams and fertile valleys, which provide a diversity of habitat for coyotes, bobcats, black bears, white-tailed deer, wild turkeys and hundreds of hawks, owls and songbirds. The agricultural areas of the Great Valley on the eastern side of the region and the farmlands to the south contribute to the diversity of the region.

The ridges and valleys of this region are a result of differences in their parent rock. Soft limestone and shale erode faster than the more resistant conglomerates and sandstone, creating ridges and valleys. These differences affect the types of plants and animals that live here.

American Goldfinch
PHOTO BY STEVE BYLAND

Double-crested Cormorant

Mixed-oak forests dominate the ridges and provide abundant food for wild-life. White-tailed deer, black bears and wild turkeys are a few of the species that feed on the ridges' abundant acorns, beech nuts, hickory nuts, wild grapes and blueberries. Migratory neotropical birds thrive in these upland forests, feasting on insects and berries.

Many rivers and streams flow through the limestone valleys, providing ideal water conditions for brook trout, New Jersey's only native trout. Glacial lakes provide a home for larger game fish, including northern pike. Northern copperheads and timber rattlesnakes, New Jersey's only venomous snakes, seek out rocky outcroppings for temporary shelter and winter dens.

Pileated Woodpecker

PHOTO BY STEVE BYLAND

Description

The Delaware Water Gap is an amazing geological formation, a large break in the Kittatinny Ridge of the Appalachian Mountains through which the Delaware River flows. Much of the land north of the water gap was purchased to create a huge water reservoir which was never built. Now a national recreation area stretches for 37 miles along the northern reaches of the Delaware River in both New Jersey and Pennsylvania. The Kittatinny Ridge Viewing Area includes the Delaware Water Gap National Recreation Area, Worthington State Forest, Stokes State Forest, High Point State Park and Walpack and Flatbrook-Roy Wildlife Management Areas.

Start with a climb to the top of Mt. Tammany in Worthington State Forest for a spectacular view of the water gap and surrounding mountains. From there, hike the several miles to Sunfish Pond, a glacial lake on top of the ridge. Work your way north along Old Mine Road and explore bottomland forests along the Delaware River, hike through deciduous forest, or paddle one of the many lakes. Experience the coolness of a hemlock ravine, the boisterous tumble of a pristine mountain stream, the sense of wilderness that comes from being surrounded by miles of unbroken forest, or being at eye-level with a turkey vulture soaring on a thermal (a rising current of warm air). Old farms still dot the valleys and the historic village of Millbrook is brought to life through living history demonstrations. Sunrise Mountain in Stokes State Forest has one of New Jersey's best views of the fall raptor migration and the view of three states from High Point State Park is inspiring.

RIDGE AND VALLEY ≡ Kittatinny Ridge Viewing Area

Premier
★ SITE ★

Wildlife to Watch

Visitors can see black bear, white-tailed deer, porcupine, striped skunk, river otter, coyote, beaver and with luck, bobcat. Reptiles and amphibians include eastern box turtle, painted turtle, northern copperhead, the endangered timber rattlesnake, red-spotted newt and American toad. Bird life is unrivaled, with northern breeding species, including common raven, hermit thrush and dark-eyed junco. Waterfowl migrate through the river valley each spring and fall. The Poxono boat launch area offers a great view of the river and Poxono Island, where bald eagles roost in winter and osprey are seen from April through September.

White-tailed deer, wild turkeys and black bears can often be seen from roads or trails. They feed on the acorns and hickory nuts of this mixed-oak forest. In winter, look for purple finch, pine siskin and common redpoll in the evergreen stands. Late May to early July is the best time to see nesting pileated woodpeckers, cliff swallows, golden-crowned kinglets, solitary vireos and Blackburnian warblers.

The Flatbrook River is one of New Jersey's premier trout streams. The crystal clear waters, filtered by thousands of acres of forest and wetlands, support a delicate web of aquatic life that trout depend upon for food. Both active dams and abandoned beaver meadows can be seen along the Big Flatbrook. Beaver-created wetlands are used by many wildlife species, including muskrats, mink, heron and bitterns. Mallard, wood duck and American black duck also thrive in these small freshwater wetlands, as do many reptiles and amphibians.

Several glacial lakes are worth exploring, including Blue Mountain and Crater Lakes. Several pull-offs along Skyline Drive offer breathtaking views of the valley below. These ridgetop overlooks also provide excellent opportunities to view the fall hawk migration. Look for sharp-shinned, broad-winged and red-shouldered hawks. Explore the ridgetop barrens along the Appalachian Trail for Edwards' hairstreak butterfly in June and buck moth in October.

Stokes State Forest features an eastern hemlock forest located on the steep slopes carved by the rushing waters of Tillman Brook. Several trails wander through this spectacular ravine, providing views of Buttermilk Falls and ferns clinging to rock crevices.

The 850-acre Dryden Kuser Natural Area in High Point State Park includes a distinctive cedar bog, the northernmost in New Jersey, with many plants that are more typical of New England than New Jersey. Walk the 2.5-mile loop trail around the bog to view more than 30 species of birds.

Trails

Miles of trails, both marked and unmarked, traverse the ridgetops and valleys. Stop at the park offices or check each website for trail maps and information.

RIDGE AND VALLEY ■ Kittatinny Ridge Viewing Area

This is a rugged area and many trails require a moderate to high level of physical stamina.

Site Notes   Most of these areas (except the Wildlife Management Areas) have restrooms and drinking water from April through October. Some roads are closed in winter. Call or check the websites for information. Hunting is allowed on most areas during prescribed seasons.

Size   Delaware Water Gap National Recreation Area: 70,000 acres

Worthington State Forest: 6,584 acres

Stokes State Forest: 16,067 acres

High Point State Park: 15,827 acres

Flatbrook-Roy WMA: 2,090 acres

Walpack WMA: 388 acres

Directions   From I-80, take exit 1 (last exit in NJ) onto Old Mine Road. Turn left at the end of the exit ramp and follow the road to Kittatinny Point Visitor Center. From there, turn around and travel north on Old Mine Road for access to other viewing areas.

Nearest Town   Columbia

Ownership   Delaware Water Gap National Recreation Area: National Park Service

Worthington State Forest

Stokes State Forest

High Point State Park: NJDEP Division of Parks and Forestry

Flatbrook-Roy WMA and Walpack WMA: NJDEP Division of Fish and Wildlife

Contact   Delaware Water Gap National Recreation Area: 570-828-2253 or 908-496-4458; www.nps.gov/DEWA/

Worthington State Forest: 908-841-9575

Stokes State Forest: 973-948-3820

High Point State Park: 973-875-4800; www.njparksandforests.org

Flatbrook-Roy WMA and Walpack WMA: 973-383-0918; www.njfishandwildlife.com

Features   trails, restrooms, drinking water, hiking, biking, cross-country skiing, interpretive center, visitor center, interpretive programs, camping, canoeing/kayaking, fee, scenic overlooks

Premier
★ SITE ★

Jenny Jump State Forest

Description

Jenny Jump's topography was shaped by geologic forces that have been active for billions of years. The forest's rock outcroppings are some of the oldest on earth; they formed deep underground and were lifted and exposed during the intercontinental collision. The glaciers of the Wisconsin Ice Age, 21,000 years ago, ground down the mountain peaks and gouged out valleys, leaving behind moraines (glacial deposits), kettle holes (a shallow body of water) and glacial erratics (rocks or boulders transported by a glacier). The ancient rolling terrain provides spectacular vistas of the Kittatinny Mountains to the west and Great Meadows, an ancient glacial lake, to the east.

Wildlife to Watch

The Jenny Jump forest complex is largely contiguous and consists of mixed-hardwood forest and forested wetlands. The area supports an impressive number of forest-nesting birds such as broad-winged hawks, pileated woodpeckers, wood thrush, veerys, hooded and Canada warblers, wild turkeys and black-billed cuckoos to name a few. Black bears also inhabit the area along with white-tailed deer, raccoons and gray squirrels. Take a hike during spring migration to see and hear a myriad of wood warblers, nuthatches, tanagers and thrushes. Scan the Great Meadows for shorebirds in the fall. Take a trip to Ghost Lake and Mountain Lake in late winter and early spring to look for waterfowl. Look for snakes sunning themselves on rocky outcrops in spring and fall.

RIDGE AND VALLEY ▫ *Jenny Jump State Forest*

Great
▲ SITE ▲

Audubon
IMPORTANT
BIRD AREAS

Trails

Nine miles of hiking trails and three miles of hiking and mountain bike trails offer magnificent views of the mountains and scenic Mountain Lake. The Summit Trail, at an elevation of 1,090 feet, offers a view of the Pequest Valley.

Site Notes The Greenwood Observatory, run by the United Astronomy Clubs of NJ, offers public programs Saturday evenings from April to October. Call for its event schedule. Parts of Jenny Jump State Forest are open for hunting during prescribed seasons.

Size 4,288 acres

Directions Take exit 12 on I-80. Go south on CR 521 and travel 1.2 miles. Turn left at the light in Hope onto CR 519 then take the first right turn onto CR 611 (Great Meadows-Hope Road). Travel 2.4 miles to Far View Road and turn left. The park office entrance is 1.7 miles on the right.

Nearest Town Hope

Ownership NJDEP Division of Parks and Forestry

Contact 908-459-4366; www.njparksandforests.org

Features restrooms, camping, fishing, boating, boat launch, canoeing/kayaking, hunting, trails

Black Bear   PHOTO BY JOHN PARKE

RIDGE AND VALLEY ▪ Jenny Jump State Forest

Great
▲ SITE ▲

29

Forest Riverine Ecosystem   PHOTO BY JOHN PARKE

Description

Kittatinny Valley State Park encompasses almost 4,000 acres of forests, fields, freshwater wetlands, glacial lakes and vernal pools located in a scenic spur of the Great Appalachian Valley. It includes Lake Aeroflex, which at 100 feet is New Jersey's deepest natural lake. This narrow valley is home to one of the most important limestone wetland communities in the state. The plants and animals that inhabit this unique ecosystem are adapted to the alkaline, nutrient-poor soils found here. Nearly 700 species of plants and 224 species of birds have been identified in the park.

Wildlife to Watch

The mosaic of habitats provides a home for a variety of mammals, including the eastern chipmunk, white-tailed deer, black bear, raccoon, skunk, oppossum and coyote. Look for signs of more elusive wildlife like scent mounds of river otter or tracks of mink along waterways. Fish species such as bluegill, largemouth bass, pickerel, perch and crappie live in the park's lakes. While no improved boat-launching facilities exist, canoeing and kayaking are popular ways to view the variety of wildlife using the lakes and ponds.

The diversity of habitats makes the park a haven for birds and bird watchers alike. Osprey and bald eagles, along with wading birds like great blue herons and snowy egrets, often fish the lakes. The woods are alive with the raucous calls of pileated, red-bellied and hairy woodpeckers and the more melodious tunes of wood thrushes and veerys. Scan the field edges for sparrows in the winter and migrant warblers in spring and fall.

Trails

Several miles of trails, both linear and looping, vary in difficulty and terrain from easy to difficult. Single track trails and gravel roads are suitable for hiking, mountain biking, cross-country skiing, snowshoeing and horseback riding. A 2-mile self-guided nature trail provides a brief introduction to the park's natural and cultural resources. Two rail-trails pass through the park: the 27-mile Paulinskill Valley Trail and the 20-mile Sussex Branch Trail. Parts of these trails are suitable for persons with disabilities. The Sussex Branch Trail connects Kittatinny Valley State Park with Allamuchy Mountain State Park and Paulinskill WMA.

Site Notes	Be sure to stop by the butterfly and hummingbird garden behind the park office. The garden was planted with native plants and serves as a living interpretive display. The park offers an array of interpretive programs year-round. Parts of the park are open for hunting during prescribed seasons.
Size	3,641 acres
Directions	From exit 25 on I-80, drive north on US 206 through Andover Borough. Turn right onto Goodale Road and follow it 1 mile to the park entrance on the right.
Nearest Town	Andover
Ownership	NJDEP Division of Parks and Forestry
Contact	973-786-6445; www.njparksandforests.org
Features	restrooms, parking, hiking, fishing, hunting, picnicking, bicycling, horseback riding, canoeing/kayaking

Eastern Chipmunk

PHOTO BY JIM MALLMAN

Great
▲ SITE ▲

Merrill Creek Reservoir

Description

The 650-acre Merrill Creek Reservoir on Scotts Mountain was constructed to store water for release into the Delaware River during periods of low flow. Surrounded by more than 2,000 acres of forest and fields, the reservoir is a 290-acre wildlife preserve, with 5 miles of hiking trails through oak forests, open fields, abandoned orchards and stands of spruce and pine.

The visitor center offers a spectacular view of the reservoir and surrounding landscape. A variety of exhibits depict historical, cultural, operational and environmental features of the preserve. A bird-feeding station located outside the picture windows, and a fireplace, spotting scope and sitting area inside make this a great place to view wildlife in comfort on cold days. Don't forget to visit the demonstration butterfly/hummingbird garden in the summer. The center offers an interactive computer kiosk, a weather station and a "kids' corner."

Wildlife to Watch

The Hawk Migration Association of North America runs a hawk watch here each fall. Bald and golden eagle, northern harrier, sharp-shinned, Cooper's and red-tailed hawks, American kestrel, merlin and northern goshawk have all been counted here. A pair of bald eagles has nested on the reservoir for more than 10 years.

Merrill Creek's location on top of Scotts Mountain assures that it receives both spring and fall migrants along the ridgetop. Most of the birds that pass

RIDGE AND VALLEY ▪ Merrill Creek Reservoir

Great
▲ SITE ▲

through New Jersey can be found here. In winter there are often thousands of snow geese on the reservoir, creating a deafening sound. Scan the reservoir for divers like bufflehead, merganser, scaup, scoter, common goldeneye and occasionally, Barrow's goldeneye. Both common and red-throated loon are frequent visitors. Walk the trails through the fields and woods in spring to see and hear scarlet tanagers, eastern wood-pewee, Baltimore oriole, great-crested flycatcher, yellow-throated and red-eyed vireo, veery, wood thrush, tree swallow, field sparrow, indigo bunting, worm-eating warbler and cerulean warbler. Black bear wander through occasionally and coyote, raccoon, striped skunk, gray squirrel and white-tailed deer may be glimpsed in any season. Reptiles and amphibians include spring peeper, wood frog, eastern box turtle, snapping turtle, black rat snakes and garter snakes.

Trails

The 5.5-mile perimeter trail offers excellent views of fall and winter waterfowl. There are two observation blinds, one along the shoreline and the other on the edge of a field. The Eagle Trail is 0.3-mile long and barrier-free. Trail maps are available at the center or online.

Site Notes The visitor center is open seven days a week with the exception of major holidays. Call or check the website for event schedule. Limited hunting is allowed during prescribed seasons.

Size 3,000 acres

Directions From westbound I-78, take exit 4 and turn right (north) on CR 637 (Stewartsville Road). Travel 1.8 miles to a blinker light and turn right onto CR 638 (Washington Street). Go 2.4 miles to intersection with NJ 57. Go diagonally across NJ 57 onto Montana Road. Travel 2 miles and bear left at a "Y" intersection. In 0.3 mile, turn left on Merrill Creek Road. Bear right on road toward the visitor center.

Nearest Town Washington

Ownership Merrill Creek Owners Group; Merrill Creek Visitor Center

Contact 908-454-1213; www.merrillcreek.com

Features interpretive center, interpretive programs, boat launch, canoeing/kayaking, trails, hiking, cross-country skiing

Snow Geese   PHOTO BY STEVE BYLAND

Great
▲ SITE ▲

Pequest WMA   PHOTO BY MIRIAM DUNNE/NJDFW

Description

The Pequest Trout Hatchery and Natural Resource Education Center was built in the 1980s to raise trout for the state's popular trout fishery. Brook, brown and rainbow trout are raised and stocked throughout the state each spring and fall. Self-guided hatchery tours let visitors view the process up close; interactive exhibits in the Natural Resource Education Center teach about trout, wildlife and local geology, and interpretive programs are offered. Visitors can view a backyard wildlife habitat demonstration area and a butterfly garden used by a variety of butterflies, moths, hummingbirds, bluebirds, tree swallows, songbirds and honeybees. The center is open weekdays except holidays.

Habitats at Pequest include ponds, river bottomland and mountain brooks, fallow and agricultural fields and upland forests. Previously much of this site was farmland; today, approximately 200 acres of the area are leased to local farmers to grow crops. The combination of upland and streamside forests, brushy old fields, emerging forests and active cropland supports a great diversity of wildlife.

Wildlife to Watch

The area's farmland and forest-edge animals include ring-necked pheasants, raccoons, woodchucks, eastern cottontails and coyotes. Look for American goldfinches and eastern bluebirds in the fields along the red trail. Bluebirds are insect-eaters and begin their nesting season in March. Goldfinches eat seeds and wait until July to nest, when a favorite plant, thistle, is available to provide

Great
▲ SITE ▲

nesting material and seeds for food. Look for the bat and bluebird houses near the center.

Come and be serenaded by spring peepers and wood frogs in early spring. Look for the bright red flash of a male cardinal staking out his breeding territory. Other birds of spring include gray catbird, willow flycatcher, white-eyed vireo, prairie and blue-winged warblers and indigo bunting. As spring progresses, migrating waterfowl can be seen on the ponds and river, the woods ring with the calls of forest birds, and woodchucks and black bears come out of hibernation. White-tailed deer fatten up on new spring growth and reptiles and amphibians look for mates. The threatened wood turtle is thought to live and breed along the Pequest River. Many species of birds nest here, including scarlet tanager, rose-breasted grosbeak, brown thrasher and wild turkey. Fall brings a profusion of color and an infusion of migrants. Osprey can be observed in spring through late fall over the hatchery.

Trails

Three marked trails run through the WMA. The 1.1-mile red interpretive trail begins at the picnic area and winds through farm fields and early successional areas. The red trail links up with the 0.9-mile yellow trail and 1.9-mile blue trail. The red trail is easy to moderate, but the blue and yellow trails each have some steep, rugged sections. The yellow trail climbs the ridge while the blue trail runs just below along a glacial formation called an esker (a ridge produced by a glacier). A rail-trail runs for several miles along the Pequest River making for easy walking and a scenic viewing experience. A trail brochure is available at the center or online at www.njfishandwildlife.com/pdf/peqtrails.pdf.

Site Notes	The center is open daily except holidays. Pequest is open for hunting during prescribed seasons.
Size	4,805 acres
Directions	From I-80, take exit 19 and travel south on CR 517. Drive 5 miles to Hackettstown. Turn right onto US 46 west and travel 8 miles to the hatchery entrance on the left.
Nearest Town	Oxford
Ownership	NJDEP Division of Fish and Wildlife
Contact	908-637-4125; www.njfishandwildlife.com
Features	interpretive center, interpretive programs, trails, hiking, biking, restrooms, drinking water, interpretive signs, cross-country skiing

Great
▲ SITE ▲

Lotus Blossoms   PHOTO BY JOHN PARKE

Description

Established in 1914 as New Jersey's first state park, Swartswood is well known for its great fishing and tranquil surroundings. Little Swartswood and Swartswood Lakes, formed by glaciers thousands of years ago, are now home to a variety of fish and wildlife. Whether viewing from land or water, there is always a chance you will catch a glimpse of spectacular wildlife, from bald eagles to the unique plant life found in the sinkhole ponds.

Wildlife to Watch

Swartswood Lake State Park is all about waterbirds and viewing is especially good fall through spring. Start at the bathing beach and scan the lake to locate birds; a spotting scope is useful. Several parking areas around both lakes provide decent vantage points. Look for pied-billed and horned grebes, double-crested cormorants, lesser scaup, ruddy duck, ring-necked duck, bufflehead and common goldeneye. Occasionally redhead, long-tailed duck and canvasback make an appearance. Little Swartswood, Duck Pond and Spring Lake attract a good number of birds as well, especially dabblers like American wigeon, American black duck, gadwall, wood duck and American coot. In spring and summer the wetlands in the park are abuzz with birds and frogs. Look and listen for bullfrogs, green frogs, spring peepers and northern chorus frogs, Acadian and willow flycatcher, Virginia rail, green heron, Canada warbler and northern waterthrush.

Great
▲ SITE ▲

Trails

The 0.6-mile Duck Pond Multi-Use Trail is a paved path with a level surface and is accessible for persons with disabilities. The trail meanders through a forested area along Duck Pond and features wayside exhibits. A bird blind allows views of birdlife with little disturbance to the habitat.

The moderately difficult 2.8-mile Spring Lake Trail begins at the end of the paved Duck Pond Trail. Follow the white markers along the natural hilly terrain through a secondary succession forest to secluded Spring Lake.

The 0.8-mile Bear Claw Trail is marked in yellow and begins at the Duck Pond parking area just to the right of the kiosk. The trail ends where it meets the paved Duck Pond Trail, allowing you to combine the two trails for a full loop back to the parking area.

The 1.5-mile Grist Mill Loop Trail is located at the southern end of Swartswood Lake by the dam. The steep rocky terrain makes this a moderate to difficult hike with rewarding views of Swartswood Lake.

Size	2,472 acres
Directions	From exit 25 on I-80 take US 206 north for approximately 12 miles. Turn left to continue on US 206 through Newton (Spring Street). Turn right at traffic light, still on US 206, and take the next left onto CR 519 (Mill Street). In 600 yds, turn left onto CR 622 and follow for 4.3 miles. Turn left onto CR 619 south and travel 0.6 mile to park entrance on right.
	To get to Little Swartswood Lake: Follow directions above to CR 622. At intersection of CR 622 and CR 619, continue straight on CR 622 for 0.4 mile to parking area on right.
Nearest Town	Newton
Ownership	NJDEP Division of Parks and Forestry
Contact	973-383-5230; www.njparksandforests.org
Features	parking, restrooms, boat launch, canoeing/kayaking, camping, picnicking, hiking, trails, cross-country skiing

Green Frog   PHOTO BY STEVE BYLAND

Great
▲ SITE ▲

Wood Duck

PHOTO BY STEVE BYLAND

Description

Wallkill National Wildlife Refuge lies along a 9-mile stretch of the Wallkill River within the Great Valley, which is bordered by the Kittatinny Mountains on the west and the Highlands Mountains to the east. Because of these features, many migratory birds are "funneled" through the Wallkill Valley. The Wallkill River bottomland is one of the few large areas of high-quality waterfowl habitat remaining in northwestern New Jersey. The refuge provides critical habitat for American black ducks, mallards, green-winged teal, wood ducks and Canada geese. The refuge straddles two major migration corridors for waterfowl that stop to rest and feed along the wetlands of the Wallkill River. Raptors and songbirds are plentiful during spring and fall migration. More than 225 species of birds use the refuge, including waterfowl, waterbirds, raptors and songbirds. The most common mammals are eastern cottontails, gray squirrels, raccoons, beavers, muskrats, red and gray foxes, eastern coyotes and white-tailed deer. Occasionally black bears and bobcats pass through the valley.

Wildlife to Watch

The 1.5-mile Wood Duck Trail traverses a mix of wetland forest, wet meadow and emergent wetlands on its path to the Wallkill River. Wetland reclamation has been accelerated here by beaver activity; note the dams and beaver lodges along the trail. Deeper water caused by beaver activity attracts muskrats, river otter, mink, great blue and green heron, American and least bittern, wood duck, mallard, American black duck, Canada goose, northern shoveler and common moorhen. The shallow areas attract spotted and solitary sandpiper

RIDGE AND VALLEY ▫ *Wallkill National Wildlife Refuge*

Great
▲ SITE ▲

and the occasional American golden plover or buff-breasted sandpiper. The wet meadows and shrubs are good places to find American woodcock, eastern phoebe, common yellowthroat, yellow warbler, indigo bunting, willow and Acadian flycatchers and rough-winged and bank swallows.

Upland grasslands provide important habitat for a variety of raptors and song-birds, including threatened grasshopper sparrows, savannah sparrows, endangered vesper sparrows and upland sandpipers. Other grassland species of note include short-eared owl, snowy owl, rough-legged hawk and northern shrike.

Trails

Nearly six miles of trails wind through the various habitats of the refuge, including the Wood Duck Nature Trail, a rail-trail running to the Wallkill River. Most of the trails cover easy terrain and are less than two miles long but can be combined for longer walks. The Appalachian Trail runs through the northern portion of the refuge. Refuge maps showing trails can be downloaded from the website.

Size	Nearly 7,500 acres
Directions	From Sussex Borough, take NJ 23 south for 2 miles. Turn left onto CR 565 north (CR 565 joins NJ 23 for 1 mile before turning north) and travel 1.4 miles to the refuge office on the left.
Nearest Town	Sussex
Ownership	U.S. Fish and Wildlife Service
Contact	973-702-7266; www.fws.gov/northeast/wallkillriver/
Features	visitor center, interpretive center, trails, restrooms, drinking water, interpretive programs, hiking, biking, cross-country skiing, canoeing/kayaking, observation platforms, scenic overlooks

Raccoon PHOTO BY STEVE BYLAND

Great
▲ SITE ▲

Allamuchy Mountain State Park 8

Description

Allamuchy Mountain State Park contains a delightful mix of upland habitats and historic sites located in a rugged, picturesque landscape. Allamuchy Natural Area, once part of the Stuyvesant Estate, is tucked away up a gravel road providing a quiet escape from the hustle and bustle of city life.

Wildlife to Watch

Walk the trail around Allamuchy or Deer Park Ponds from fall through spring for a good variety of migrating and wintering waterfowl and songbirds. Look for raccoon, mink and weasel tracks in the mud or snow, particularly along the many water courses. Boating on any of the lakes is a great way to get close to wildlife.

Audubon
IMPORTANT
BIRD AREAS

Trails

There are 14 miles of marked trails and 20 miles of unmarked trails varying in difficulty from moderate to rugged. A 3-mile section of the Sussex Branch Rail-Trail winds through the park from Waterloo Road to Cranberry Lake.

Site Notes: Parts of Allamuchy Mountain State Park are open for hunting during prescribed seasons.

Size: 8,815 acres

Directions: Park office: from exit 25 on I-80, travel north on US 206 to CR 604 (Willow Grove Road). Turn left and travel south for 7.5 miles to park office on the right. Allamuchy Natural Area: from exit 19 on I-80, travel south on CR 517 for approximately 3 miles to Deer Park Road on the left. Take Deer Park Road (gravel road) for 1 mile to parking area at end. In summer, follow the single track lane 1 mile farther to additional parking areas.

Nearest Town: Hackettstown

Ownership: NJDEP Division of Parks and Forestry

Contact: 908-852-3790; www.njparksandforests.org

Features: parking, restrooms, boat launch, boating, camping, hunting, fishing, picnicking, hiking, biking

Bear Swamp Wildlife Management Area 9

Description

This WMA is located along the eastern slope of the Kittatinny Ridge and largely consists of mixed-hardwood/coniferous swamp forest and upland hardwood forest of oak, beech and sugar maple. This large unbroken forest tract provides critically important breeding and nesting habitat for several interior forest species. Additional habitats include fallow fields in various stages of succession.

Wildlife to Watch

It is possible to catch a rare glimpse of the northern goshawk deep in the forest here. Other raptors include broad-winged, sharp-shinned and red-shouldered hawks and barred owls. Listen and look for cerulean and black-throated green warblers, veery, red-headed woodpeckers and northern parulas in spring and summer. The name "Bear Swamp" was aptly given as black bear inhabit the area along with bobcat, white-tailed deer, raccoon and mink. Several species of wood-dwelling moths and butterflies can be found as well.

Audubon
IMPORTANT
BIRD AREAS

Trails

Several miles of unmarked trails traverse the WMA. Trails are mostly easy to moderate but not always easy to find.

Site Notes: This is a natural area with no facilities. Bear Swamp is open for hunting during prescribed seasons.

Size: 2,906 acres

Directions: From Route 206 in Branchville take CR 633 (Kemah Lake Road) west for approximately 1.5 miles to parking area on right. For additional exploration points, park at either end of Stempert Road (off CR 655 or CR 521) and walk the old road bed.

Nearest Town: Branchville

Ownership: NJDEP Division of Fish and Wildlife

Contact: 973-383-0918; www.njfishandwildlife.com

Features: parking

Johnsonburg Swamp Preserve 10

Description

Johnsonburg Swamp Preserve is a stellar example of a limestone forest, a unique habitat type dominated by sugar maple. Limestone outcroppings provide scenic overlooks of Mystery Pond and the complex of wooded wetlands that serve as home to many rare and endangered plants and animals.

Wildlife to Watch

Red-shouldered hawks, barred owls and red-headed woodpeckers inhabit the forest. The overlooks provide a great vantage point for viewing the fall hawk migration. Bobcat haunt the swamp and rocky outcroppings along with black bear, gray fox and coyotes.

Trails

Seven miles of rugged but well-marked trails wind through a variety of habitats. From the parking area, hike along the field edges to the yellow trail and on to "High Point" for a magnificent view of the vast wetland community formed by an underground river welling up inside a horseshoe-shaped ridge of limestone. The trails are color-coded. The yellow trail connects to the Glen

Wyse trail and the blue trail to lead hikers to other areas of Johnsonburg and along the ridge to other viewing areas of the pond and wetland community. There are six trails in all.

Site Notes: This is a nature preserve with rare natural communities. Please stay on the trails and Leave No Trace.

Size: 780 acres

Directions: From exit 19 on I-80 go straight at end of ramp onto CR 667 north. In 0.25 mile, bear left onto CR 612. Go 5 miles to intersection with CR 519. Turn right onto CR 519 then stay straight onto CR 661. Take CR 661 to NJ 94 and turn right. In 0.5 mile, turn right onto Yellow Frame Road. The entrance to Johnsonburg Preserve is 0.25 mile on the right. Park in the field by the gate.

Nearest Town: Newton/Blairstown

Ownership: The Nature Conservancy

Contact: 908-879-7262, www.nature.org/wherewework/northamerica/states/newjersey/

Features: trails, parking

Paulinskill Wildlife Management Area/ Hyper Humus Marshes 11

Description

The ponds of the Hyper Humus tract were formed in the 1900s by peat and humus mining. A limestone fen represents a rare ecosystem and offers a chance to observe unique plants. The wetlands are dominated by cattails, pear hawthorn, rush aster and bog rosemary.

Wildlife to Watch

More than 200 species of birds have been recorded at this site. The diversity of habitats, including forested wetlands, emergent marsh and open water, provides breeding, nesting and resting habitat for rare species such as American bitterns, pied-billed grebes, common moorhens, red-shouldered hawks and long-eared owls. The area serves as a staging area for migrating waterfowl and shorebirds in spring and fall. Beaver, muskrat and river otter are at home in the river and marsh. Amphibians and reptiles abound, as do butterflies and dragonflies.

Audubon
IMPORTANT
BIRD AREAS

Trails

Both the Paulinskill Valley and Sussex Branch rail-trails make up part of the 2-mile, unmarked loop-trail that skirts the impoundments and makes for an easy walk with lots of viewing opportunities. There are restroom facilities located by the Paulinskill Valley trail.

Site Notes: This is a natural area with few facilities. Paulinskill WMA is open for hunting during prescribed seasons.

Size: 1,907 acres

Directions: From the intersections of US 206 and NJ 94 north of Newton, travel east on NJ 94 for 1.4 miles to the entrance on your right. Follow the gravel drive to the parking area.

Nearest Town: Newton

Ownership: NJDEP Division of Fish and Wildlife

Contact: 973-383-0918; www.njfishandwildlife.com

Features: trails, parking, restrooms, canoeing/kayaking, hiking

White Lake Wildlife Management Area 12

Description

White Lake contains numerous habitats unique to this part of New Jersey. These include White Lake, the wetlands surrounding parts of the lake, a fen at the eastern end, a limestone forest, old fields and a small section of hemlock forest. Many unusual plants such as walking fern, pitcher plants, slender yellow lady's slippers and yellow (chinkapin) oak occur here due to the mineral-rich soils located near the old marlworks. The historic Vass house on the property is built from local limestone. The lake gets its name from its white bottom—a characteristic of the calcium-rich clay called marl that lines the lake.

Wildlife to Watch

Look for wintering long-eared owls, great blue herons and a variety of water-fowl. The calcium-rich soil produces rare and interesting plants that attract rare butterflies, including meadow fritillaries, Baltimore checkerspot and northern metalmark butterflies.

Trails

A trail system is being developed by Warren County in partnership with the Nature Conservancy. The Ridge and Valley Trail starts at Spring Valley Road and circles the eastern side of the tract, ending on Route 521. From the trail you can observe the marl works, ice house, lime kiln and old hunting cabin.

Site Notes: This is a natural area with no facilities. White Lake WMA is open for hunting during prescribed seasons.

Size: 961 acres

Directions: From exit 12 on I-80 take CR 521 north for approximately 8 miles to entrance and parking area on the right.

Nearest Town: Blairstown

Ownership: NJDEP Division of Fish and Wildlife; County of Warren

Contact: 973-383-0918; www.njfishandwildlife.com
908-453-3252; www.co.warren.nj.us

Features: canoeing/kayaking, fishing, parking

RIDGE AND VALLEY Other Sites

Other sites

Whittingham Wildlife Management Area

13

Description

Whittingham's extensive freshwater marsh and diverse upland forests and fields are home to a variety of wildlife. This wetland complex is the headwater of the Pequest River. Numerous springs originate deep within the limestone bedrock. The springs' calcium-rich water bubbles to the surface and sustains the wetlands. Whittingham Wildlife Management Area is one of northern New Jersey's most pristine upland forests. For this reason, early settlers cleared these areas first and farmed them. Today much of the wildlife management area is naturally revegetating to a sugar maple mixed-hardwood forest ecosystem.

The limestone deposits found here are all the evidence that is left of a great inland ocean that once covered much of the eastern seaboard. When this ancient sea drained, the ocean floor was layered with the shells and skeletons of the many aquatic creatures left behind by the receding waters. Their remains were compacted to form the limestone bedrock, bluffs and other outcrops that you see here and at other sites in north Jersey.

Wildlife to Watch

Walk along the edge of the marsh to look for beavers, river otters and other wetlands wildlife. Many species of waterfowl are present in different seasons, including nesting wood ducks, American black ducks and mallards. Several different species of turtle reside in the freshwater marsh as well, including snapping, wood and eastern painted turtles. While exploring the forests you may encounter the ruffed grouse (best known for its explosive flushes when approached too closely). Listen for the reverberating drumming sound males produce to attract mates in the spring. Many kinds of wildlife flourish here because of the limestone rock and calcium-rich soil. The limestone is also home to many species of amphibians such as wood frogs, spring peepers, American toads and spotted salamanders, that live and breed in ephemeral pools in the forest.

Trails

There are no marked trails.

Site Notes: The Whittingham Wildlife Management Area is a natural area with no facilities. It is open for hunting during prescribed seasons.

Size: 1,930 acres

Directions: From the junction of US 206 and CR 611, take CR 611 west for approximately 1 mile to the wetland overlook on the right. From the overlook, go back to US 206 and turn left. Take the next left onto CR 618. Proceed 1.4 miles and turn left onto Springdale Road. Proceed 0.2 mile to the parking area on the left. The trail from the parking area goes through the natural area to Big Spring wetlands.

Nearest Town: Newton

Ownership: NJDEP Division of Fish, Game and Wildlife

Contact: 908-637-4125; www.njfishandwildlife.com

Features: parking, hiking, trails, restrooms

RIDGE AND VALLEY ∷ *Other Sites*

Other sites

White-tailed Deer

Female Mallard

RIDGE AND VALLEY ■ *Other Sites*

Other sites

Highlands

Premier Sites

Great Sites

Other Sites

94

20

•Franklin   17

19   23   15

206 15 28   16   21

•Andover

22   27

80   •Boonton

Dover 46

206   10

23   Morristown•

287

25
Washington   32   29   18

31   24   202   14

•Phillipsburg   •High Bridge
26   31

78

22

•Milford   30

Rugged mountain terrain, glacial lakes and spring-fed wetlands

This region of rough, mountainous terrain also has areas of rolling hills and farmland, meadows and grassland and prime beaver habitat. It contains the highest concentration of glacial lakes in the state, or the entire eastern seaboard for that matter. There are also numerous reservoirs, lakes and ponds that were created when many of the region's rivers and streams were dammed.

An array of habitats occurs on the ridges and valleys that dominate the landscape here. These include pine-oak forests, hemlock ravines, northern mixed-hardwood forests of oak, maple, birch, ash, hickory, hemlock and white pine and old farm fields and woodlots in various stages of succession. The large contiguous forest of the Highlands supports the highest concentration of birds of prey in the state. Cooper's hawks, goshawks, barred owls and red-shouldered hawks nest throughout the forests of this region, along with

Indigo Bunting   PHOTO BY STEVE BYLAND

many songbirds that rely on deep forest for successful reproduction. Large flocks of wild turkeys and herds of white-tailed deer roam the forests and fields, as do coyotes, bears and bobcats. Black bears and bobcats are denizens of the many rhododendron and mountain laurel swamps that dot the higher elevation's landscape.

The Highlands also contain thousands of acres of glacial, floodplain and spring-fed wetlands that feed its numerous streams. Beavers, otters, great blue herons and endangered and threatened species, including bog turtles and wood turtles, depend on the extensive network of wetlands, lakes and streams. This region also supports large populations of small mammals, reptiles, amphibians, butterflies, moths and dragonflies.

The Highlands region's huge areas of public land are an anomaly in New Jersey—the Great Swamp National Wildlife Refuge, Wawayanda, Ringwood, Long Pond Ironworks State Parks, the Pyramid Mountain Natural Historical Area, the 35,000-acre Pequannock Watershed (owned by the City of Newark but open by permit to the public), the Black River and Wildcat Ridge Wildlife Management Areas, and many other state, county and municipal tracts provide large expanses of contiguous natural lands. This preservation of entire ecosystems benefits wildlife and allows for extended hikes and pleasing vistas from many vantage points. Today the Highlands are relatively undisturbed, though many plants and animals remain endangered. The area is protected as the Highlands Preservation Area (a region considered to hold exceptional natural resource value) and from development and degradation under the Highlands Water Protection and Planning Act.

Visitors to this region will also delight in the many historic and cultural features that the Highlands have to offer. Rich deposits of iron led to the development of ironworks and "plantations" as early as the 1760s. Ringwood, Longpond, Andover, Oxford and numerous other locations were the sites of furnaces, forges and bloomeries, and many of the furnaces and buildings are still standing. There are also many historic sites associated with the American Revolution, including those in and around Morristown, such as Jockey Hollow and the Ford Mansion. The Morris Canal traversed the region, opening in 1823 and operating for 100 years. It left behind its inclined planes and locks in Waterloo Village and the portless towns of Port Murray and Port Colden, once stops on the canal.

Mallards

PHOTO BY JIM MALLMAN

Photo by Dwight Hiscano

Green Heron

PHOTO BY STEVE BYLAND

Description

The Great Swamp area encompasses the Great Swamp National Wildlife Refuge, the Great Swamp Outdoor Education Center of Morris County and the Somerset County Environmental Education Center at Lord Stirling Park. The Great Swamp is a remnant of the ancient Glacial Lake Passaic, which once occupied much of the current day Passaic River floodplain. Today its marshes, ponds, hardwood swamps and upland forests host a variety of wildlife.

The Great Swamp National Wildlife Refuge was established to provide migration, nesting and feeding habitat for migratory birds in an area where habitats for many species are highly fragmented due to development. Great Swamp contains more than 7,400 acres of hardwood swamp, upland timber, freshwater marsh, scrub-shrub, pasture and cropland. This diverse habitat montage attracts a wide variety of migratory and resident birds. With the continued protection of its wilderness, the National Wildlife Refuge will become increasingly important as a haven for wildlife amidst the surrounding development.

The 897-acre Lord Stirling Park, which occupies the western portion of the Great Swamp Basin, is a good place to start. Lord Stirling Park's Environmental Education Center offers an 8.5-mile trail system, including 2.5 miles of board-walk, allowing easy access to wetter portions of the park. Naturalists are available to answer questions and provide information, and an extensive range of programs is offered.

Explore the 40-acre Great Swamp Outdoor Education Center located in the eastern portion of the Great Swamp adjoining the National Wildlife Refuge. There are guided nature walks of the center and in the refuge. Inside the

HIGHLANDS ■ Great Swamp Viewing Area

Premier
★ SITE ★

center are informative exhibits, interactive games for kids, trail guides and listings of programs.

All three sites offer special events, exhibits and interpretive programs about the wildlife and habitats of the area. Educational programs enrich the visitor experience through increased understanding of the swamp's ecosystem.

Wildlife to Watch

The Great Swamp hosts over 200 species of birds over the course of a year, and nearly 90 species raise their young here. The best season to see marsh and water birds in the Great Swamp is during early spring migration before vegetation emerges and conceals them. The refuge has great populations of nesting wood ducks and bluebirds, thanks to hundreds of nest boxes maintained for both species. Other noteworthy residents are red-shouldered hawks, red-tailed hawks, barred owls and great blue herons. Summer also offers good wildlife-viewing opportunities, including biting insects! Dress appropriately and bring insect repellent.

The swamp contains many old oak and beech trees, red maple, stands of mountain laurel and species of other plants from both the northern and southern botanical zones. Expect to see or hear yellow-billed cuckoo, white-eyed vireo, five species of woodpecker, black-and-white warbler, brown creeper, scarlet tanager and American redstart in the forested areas. Mammals include white-tailed deer, river otters, muskrats, raccoons, skunks, eastern chipmunks, red foxes, woodchucks, gray squirrels, opossums and eastern cottontails. There is an interesting variety of fish, reptiles and amphibians, including wood turtles, eastern and midland painted turtles and endangered bog turtles. The refuge is one of the few places in the state where the endangered blue-spotted salamander still exists.

The western half of the National Wildlife Refuge is intensively managed to maintain optimum habitat for a wide variety of wildlife. Water levels are regulated, grasslands and brush are mowed periodically to maintain habitat and species diversity, shrubs are planted, nesting structures are provided, and other habitat management practices are employed. Public access in this area is limited to the Wildlife Observation Center and Pleasant Plains Road to minimize disturbance of wildlife.

Numerous wetland raptors inhabit the swamp. Look closely to catch a glimpse of the courtship rituals of barred owls or red-shouldered hawks. If water levels are low in the swamp, look to see various sandpipers including greater and lesser yellowlegs and solitary, spotted and least sandpipers.

Audubon
IMPORTANT
BIRD AREAS

HIGHLANDS ■ *Great Swamp Viewing Area*

Trails

All three viewing sites have trail systems running throughout their respective land. Some trails are universally accessible. The NWR offers the opportunity for longer hikes over more primitive trails. It also features a wildlife auto-tour route. Maps of all three sites are available online or at the respective visitor centers.

Site Notes   Great Swamp National Wildlife Refuge is open for limited hunting. The NWR headquarters is open weekdays. The Great Swamp Outdoor Education Center and the Somerset County Environmental Education Center are open seven days a week.

Size   Great Swamp National Wildlife Refuge: 7,500 acres

Morris County Center: 40 acres

Somerset County Center: 950 acres

Directions   From I-287 exit 30A (Maple Avenue), travel 3 miles to Lord Stirling Road. Turn left; Somerset County Park Commission Environmental Education Center is 1 mile farther on the left. For Great Swamp National Wildlife Refuge, continue on Lord Stirling Road (which becomes White Bridge Road). Turn left on Pleasant Plains Road and proceed through the gate to refuge headquarters on the right. For the Great Swamp Outdoor Education Center of the Morris County Park Commission, continue on Pleasant Plains Road to White Bridge Road. Turn left and proceed to New Vernon Road. Turn right and travel to Meyersville Road. Turn left and proceed 2.4 miles on Meyersville Road to Fairmount Road. Turn left on Fairmount and proceed 1.8 miles to Southern Boulevard. Turn left and go 1 mile to entrance on the left.

Nearest Town   Basking Ridge, Chatham

Ownership   National Wildlife Refuge: U.S. Fish and Wildlife Service

Contact   National Wildlife Refuge: 973-425-1222; www.fws.gov/northeast/greatswamp/

Great Swamp Outdoor Education Center: Morris County Park Commission, 973-635-6629; www.morrisparks.net

Somerset County Park Commission Environmental Education Center at Lord Stirling Park: 908-766-2489; www.somersetcountyparks.org

Features   visitor center, interpretive programs, interpretive signs, trails, hiking, restrooms, drinking water, observation blind, horseback riding

HIGHLANDS ▪ Great Swamp Viewing Area

Premier
★ SITE ★

53

Dramatic rock outcroppings make for scenic viewing

Brown Creeper

PHOTO BY BOB CUNNINGHAM

Description

Located within 35 miles of the New Jersey-New York metropolitan area, the Newark-Pequannock Watershed property represents the heart of the Highlands region. Spanning 11 municipalities, the property's five reservoirs provide water for the City of Newark and the surrounding suburbs. In addition, it provides many recreational opportunities for visitors and serves as a refuge for wildlife. The clear lakes, streams and ponds, the mountains with their dramatic rock outcroppings, the forests and the varied vegetation of the watershed all combine to make it one of the most scenic areas in New Jersey.

The Pequannock Watershed contains the Pequannock River and its major tributaries, including the Macopin River, Clinton Brook, Apshawa Brook and Pacock Brook. Most of the waters within the watershed are classified by NJDEP as Category One for their exceptional resource value and are therefore afforded New Jersey's highest protection to guard against changes in water quality. The site sits within the Highlands Preservation Area, a region considered to hold exceptional natural resource value, and is protected from development and degradation under the Highlands Water Protection and Planning Act. The forests help impede runoff, prevent erosion and assist in filtering water.

The flat-topped ridges are studded with bedrock outcrops, evidence of glaciation, as are the narrow valleys filled with a variety of unconsolidated deposits.

HIGHLANDS ▦ Newark-Pequannock Watershed

Premier ★ SITE ★

Indeed, several of the ponds, swamps and lakes in the watershed were formed by glacial activity, including Echo Lake, Hanks Pond and Cedar Pond.

This forested site contains some of the largest unfragmented forest tracts in New Jersey and is as diverse as the birds and animals that reside within. The plateaus, ridgetops and valleys support a varied range of vegetation types. There are deciduous and coniferous forests, hemlock groves and spruce plantations and mixed forests with scrub-shrub and riparian habitats. The watershed represents significant migratory stopover habitat for songbirds, raptors and some waterbirds.

Wildlife to Watch

The watershed's large unfragmented forests provide niches for numerous forest-dwelling birds and mammals. Cooper's hawk, red-shouldered hawk, barred owl, long-eared owl and northern goshawk are said to breed here—also cerulean warblers, brown creeper, least flycatcher and ruffed grouse. Scan the treetops for dozing porcupines. Wild turkeys, white-tailed deer and gray squirrels feed on the area's abundant acorns. Black bears feast on the abundant blueberries, as do raccoons, red foxes and numerous species of birds.

The reservoirs and riparian corridors provide habitat for American woodcock, great blue heron, pied-billed grebe, American bittern and Louisiana waterthrush. The watershed creates an overlap area where many northern species reach their southern limit and many southern species their northern limit.

Long-tailed Weasel

Look for winter wren, black-throated blue and Blackburnian warbler, Acadian flycatcher, yellow-throated vireo and hooded warbler.

Hawks migrate along the ridges in the fall. Park on top of Bearfort Mountain and hike the 0.5 mile to the fire tower to watch the migration. There is a rocky outcropping that makes a good viewing platform and some good ledges from which to scan the skies. Keep your eyes on the ground as you hike, particularly on exposed rocky areas on cool fall days. Both northern copperhead and the endangered timber rattlesnake inhabit the area and will come out to bask on the rocks during the day.

Trails

There are miles and miles of trails, both marked and unmarked, running through the watershed property and connecting this site to others. The terrain is varied and often steep and/or rocky. Most hikes are moderate to difficult over rough surfaces. Good maps are highly recommended. Maps are available on the NWCDC website, at the Echo Lake office, or from the NY/NJ Trail Conference.

Site Notes Access permits are required. Open for hunting during prescribed seasons. Call or visit the Echo Lake office for information and to purchase an access permit before visiting the site.

Size 35,000 acres

Directions From the junction of Interstate 287 and NJ 23, take NJ 23 north for almost 8 miles to Echo Lake Road. Turn right and travel 1 mile to the Echo Lake office on the left.

Nearest Town Newfoundland

Ownership City of Newark, managed by the Newark Watershed Conservation and Development Corporation

Contact 973-697-2850; www.newarkwatershed.com/

Features hiking, visitor center, trails, horseback riding, fee, canoe/kayaking

Long-eared Owl PHOTO BY JOHN PARKE

HIGHLANDS ▪ Newark-Pequannock Watershed

Premier ★ SITE ★

Apshawa Preserve

Take a hike around scenic Butler Lake

Apshawa Preserve

PHOTO BY JOHN PARKE

Description

This rugged 576-acre preserve contains some of New Jersey's finest intact northern hardwood forest and offers a diversity of Highlands habitats, including mixed-hardwood forest dominated by oak and sugar maple. Butler Reservoir, a scenic attraction for hikers and wildlife watchers alike, offers opportunities to see waterfowl and migrant songbirds. The Apshawa Brook flows through the preserve to the Pequannock River, providing a riparian corridor used by mammals and migrating songbirds.

Wildlife to Watch

The Apshawa Preserve is home to a great diversity of wildlife including red-shouldered hawk, barred owl and northern species such as yellow-bellied sapsuckers. Comb the riparian area along the brook for mink, long-tailed weasel and raccoon tracks. Look and listen for hermit and wood thrush, veery, tufted titmouse and black-capped chickadee.

Trails

Nearly seven miles of blazed trails traverse the Apshawa Preserve and are open seven days a week, dawn to dusk, for hiking, bicycling, horseback riding, nature study and nearby fishing. The trails are of moderate difficulty with a few steep spots, but the scenery is worth the effort.

Great
▲ SITE ▲

Site Notes This is a natural area with no facilities.

Size 576 acres

Directions Take exit 52 on I-287 to NJ 23 north. Go 5.6 miles. Turn right onto Germantown Road and go 2.5 miles. Turn right on Macopin Road and drive 1.6 miles to Northwood Road. Turn right and go 100 yards at the Apshawa Preserve sign and parking area on right.

Nearest Town West Milford

Ownership County of Passaic, NJ Conservation Foundation

Contact NJ Conservation Foundation: 908-234-1225; http://njconservation.org/html/preserves/apshawa.htm

Passaic County: 973-881-4832; www.passaiccountynj.org/ParksHistorical/Parks/apshawapreserve.htm

Features parking, trails, scenic overlooks

A pair of Tufted Titmice

PHOTO BY STEVE BYLAND

Great
▲ SITE ▲

HIGHLANDS ▦ *Apshawa Preserve*

Ringwood State Park

PHOTO BY JOHN PARKE

Description

Development of Ringwood's iron industry began in 1740. America's foremost ironmaster, Abram S. Hewitt, built Ringwood Manor, now a National Historical Landmark. The gardens surrounding Skylands Manor House are the only botanical gardens in the state park system. Notable natural habitats include a northern New Jersey shrub swamp, hardwood-conifer swamp and ridgetop communities of plants specifically adapted to the extremely dry, harsh conditions existing on rocky outcrops and cliffs.

The old stone walls, furnaces and other remnants of the once industrious ironworking community that is Long Pond Ironworks State Park, adjacent to Ringwood, now sit tranquilly next to the swiftly flowing Wanaque River. Long Pond Ironworks was founded in 1766 by German ironmaster Peter Hasenclever. Hasenclever brought 500 ironworkers and their families from Germany to build an ironworks "plantation," including a furnace, forge, houses, shops and farms. A dam at "Long Pond," now Greenwood Lake on the upper Wanaque River, provided the hydropower to operate a blast for the furnace and a large forge. A reservoir, trout stream and hemlock forest make this historical area a great wildlife-viewing site.

Wildlife to Watch

These vast, contiguous forests are good habitat for black bears, wild turkeys and endangered bobcats. Bobcats are wary of humans and are more often

Great
▲ SITE ▲

heard than seen. Bald eagles frequent the region, which is noted for its many lakes. Canada geese are plentiful around Sally's Pond near the Ringwood park office. In Long Pond Ironworks, take the trails from the parking lot by Monksville Reservoir up into the forest. Watch for porcupines, coyotes, white-tailed deer and black bears from March to December. Pileated woodpeckers, wild turkeys, red-shouldered hawks, Cooper's hawks and spring and summer warblers are just a few of the birds living here. In fall and winter, check the reservoir for waterfowl.

Trails

There are several miles of trails ranging in length from 1 to 7.5 miles with terrain from moderate to difficult. This is a rugged part of New Jersey. A trail map is available at the office or toll booth. Park at Ringwood Manor, Skylands Manor or the Monksville Reservoir parking areas to access trails.

Site Notes The area is open for hunting in designated areas during prescribed seasons.

Size 4,291 acres

Directions Ringwood State Park: From I-287, take exit 55 to CR 511. Travel north on CR 511 for 8.5 miles to Sloatsburg Road. Turn right and travel 1.5 miles to the park entrance sign. Continue for 1.1 miles to the office at Ringwood Manor.

Long Pond Ironworks: Continue north on CR 511 past Sloatsburg Road for approximately 3.5 miles to park entrance on the left.

Nearest Town Ringwood

Ownership NJDEP Division of Parks and Forestry

Contact 973-962-7031; www.njparksandforests.org

Features trails, visitor center, hiking, mountain biking, cross-country skiing, horseback riding, restrooms, picnicking, drinking water, fee, boat launch, canoeing/kayaking, food

Barred Owl   PHOTO BY JIM MALLMAN

Great
▲ SITE ▲

Scherman-Hoffman Wildlife Sanctuary

Spring and fall migration are phenomenal

Passaic River

PHOTO BY JOHN PARKE

Description

This sanctuary is primarily upland deciduous forest with a few fields and the floodplain forest along the Passaic River near its headwaters. The river here is covered by the forest canopy and remains cool enough to support wild trout in the deeper pools. The combination of ridge and river valley along a major flyway means a huge number of species of birds can be seen on any given day. Over 175 species have been recorded here, 60 of those considered breeding birds.

Wildlife to Watch

The spring and fall migration are phenomenal. This is one of the best spots to find the elusive mourning warbler. Other great finds can include olive-sided and yellow-bellied flycatchers, Kentucky and hooded warblers (both of which have nested here), winter wren and pileated woodpecker. Nesting birds include Acadian flycatcher, eastern bluebird, indigo bunting, field, song and chipping sparrows, northern mockingbird and brown thrasher. Waves of kinglets, thrushes and vireos begin arriving in September. Warblers can be seen by mid-August. Scherman-Hoffman is great for winter finches, including rarities like pine grosbeak and common redpoll.

Trails

The many trails showcase this site's variety of habitats. The 1-mile Field Loop Trail is accessible to all-terrain strollers, but there is a 100-foot change in elevation as you walk from the center to the valley floor. The 0.5-mile-long River

HIGHLANDS ▪ Scherman-Hoffman Wildlife Sanctuary

Trail winds along the Passaic River near its headwaters and provides a tranquil setting in which to look and listen for belted kingfisher, wood ducks and Louisiana waterthrush (you may need boots in spring and summer). The River Trail links to Dogwood Trail which leads upslope through deciduous woods of oak, maple, beech and tulip trees to the ridge above the center.

Site Notes	The visitor center/sanctuary office and bookstore are open daily. Call for hours. Trails are open dawn to dusk every day.
Size	276 acres
Directions	From I-287 take exit 30 B. Go straight through the traffic light (Route 202) at the end of the exit ramp. Go 0.25 mile and bear right on Hardscrabble Road. Go approximately 1 mile to the sanctuary driveway on the right where Hardscrabble Road bends 90 degrees to the left.
Nearest Town	Bernardsville
Ownership	New Jersey Audubon Society
Contact	908-766-5787; www.njaudubon.org
Features	interpretive center, interpretive programs, restrooms, observation platforms, drinking water, hiking, store

Wood Frog

PHOTO BY JOHN PARKE

HIGHLANDS *Scherman-Hoffman Wildlife Sanctuary*

Great
▲ SITE ▲

Bear tracks in snow

PHOTO BY JOHN PARKE

Description

This scenic area boasts several small lakes, Edison Bog—a wetland of significance —scrub-shrub wetlands and acres of forested uplands and ridges with overlooks affording fantastic views of the surrounding landscape. Thomas Edison owned an iron mine here, and some of the smaller mine shafts and foundations of the mining town are still visible. Edison Pond and Edison Bog are named for him.

Wildlife to Watch

Sparta Mountain is one of the only places in New Jersey where you might catch a glimpse of a golden-winged warbler. Many species of warblers breed here, including cerulean and black-throated blue. Other breeding species include wood thrushes, scarlet tanagers and blue-headed, red-eyed and yellow-throated vireos. Rose-breasted grosbeaks are fairly common. While bobcat inhabit the area, they are extremely wary and hard to see. The best opportunities are at dusk and dawn. Ryker Lake contains trophy bass. Look for circular nests in the shallows along the lake's edge in spring. Waterfowl are plentiful in spring and fall and wading birds are common in summer.

Audubon
IMPORTANT
BIRD AREAS

HIGHLANDS ■ Sparta Mountain Viewing Area

Great
▲ SITE ▲

Trails

The New York-New Jersey Trail Conference has developed trails from the Edison parking area through the sanctuary and the WMA. Look for the trail kiosk in the parking area. The Highlands Trail (marked in teal blazes) traverses a portion of the area. Trails are of moderate difficulty.

Site Notes This is a natural area with limited facilities.

Size 3,275 acres

Directions Take exit 34B on I-80 onto NJ 15 north. Go 8.5 miles and exit onto CR 517 north. Take CR 517 north for approximately 4 miles to Ogdensburg. Turn right onto Edison Road. Go 2.4 miles and turn left into the Edison parking area.

Nearest Town Sparta

Ownership NJDEP Division of Fish and Wildlife

NJ Audubon Society

Passaic River Coalition

Contact NJDEP-DFW: 973-383-0918; www.njfishandwildlife.com

NJ Audubon Society: 973-835-2160; www.njaudubon.org

Passaic River Coalition: 908-222-0315; www.passaicriver.org

Features parking, trails, hiking

Bobcat

PHOTO BY MICK VALENT/NJDFW

Great
▲ SITE ▲

Wawayanda State Park

PHOTO BY LAURIE PETTIGREW/NJDFW

Description

Enjoy the captivating scenery of the northern Highlands while hiking miles of marked trails. Located along the New York state border atop the Wawayanda Plateau, nearly a third of this park is preserved in three natural areas: Bearfort Mountain, Wawayanda Swamp and Wawayanda Hemlock Ravine. Attractions include the remains of buildings from a once-thriving iron-making village, a 19.6-mile section of the Appalachian Trail and a 1.5-mile section of boardwalk and suspension bridge over Pochuck Creek to watch songbirds, raptors and wading birds.

Wawayanda's northern hardwood forests and large patches of contiguous forested cover are very important habitat for many species of wildlife, including threatened and endangered raptors such as barred owls, Cooper's hawks and red-shouldered hawks. The long-term stewardship of the park's northern hardwood forest ecosystem is critical, as public lands are key to the long-term survival of viable populations of forest species.

Wildlife to Watch

The park is critical habitat for black bears, bobcats, porcupines, coyotes and foxes, as well as wild turkeys, ruffed grouse and pileated woodpeckers. The elusive bobcat roams the rocky ridges and hunts the forests and swamps year-round. The Division of Fish and Wildlife caught and released bobcats from New England on Bearfort Mountain in the early 1980s in an effort to restore New Jersey's dwindling population.

HIGHLANDS ▪ Wawayanda State Park

Great
▲ SITE ▲

You may have to look no further than the visitor center to see black bears from late March through December. During the winter months they hibernate in dens that they make in rhododendron thickets. Wawayanda's northern hardwood forest, with its varied terrain, meets all of a bear's needs for food and cover. In addition, the wetlands in the park are home to many less-reclusive species, including beaver, river otter and great blue heron. The park has a heron rookery, where the great blue herons nest high in the trees in large stick nests.

The Wawayanda Hemlock Ravine Natural Area is a steep, shaded hemlock forest surrounded by mixed-oak and hardwood forests. Look here to see red-eyed vireo, Blackburnian and black-throated green warblers, scarlet tanagers, black-capped chickadees and tufted titmice feeding in the forest canopy. The cool, moist floor of the ravine harbor's salamanders, moles and shrews.

Bearfort Mountain Natural Area is home to such threatened and endangered wildlife as red-shouldered hawks, barred owls, timber rattlesnakes and wood turtles.

Trails

Over 60 miles of well-marked trails cover rough and hilly terrain. The trails are not universally accessible. Trail maps are available at the park office or from the New York/New Jersey Trail Conference (www.nynjtc.org).

Site Notes	Open for hunting in designated areas during prescribed seasons.
Size	34,350 acres
Directions	From I-287 take exit 52 to NJ 23. Travel on NJ 23 north to Newfoundland and intersection of CR 513 (Union Valley Road). Go north on CR 513 for approximately 7 miles until a fork in road. Turn left and proceed on White Road 0.2 mile to Warwick Turnpike. Turn left (north) on Warwick Turnpike and travel 4 miles to park entrance on the left.
Nearest Town	West Milford
Ownership	NJDEP Division of Parks and Forestry
Contact	973-853-4462; www.njparksandforests.org
Features	restrooms, camping, parking, hiking, trails, biking, boat launch, canoeing/kayaking, food, picnicking, cross-country skiing, horseback riding, drinking water

Red Fox PHOTO BY STEVE BYLAND

Great
▲ SITE ▲

Norvin Green State Forest

PHOTO BY JOHN PARKE

Description

Explore New Jersey's spectacular Highlands region as you hike through Norvin Green State Forest. Trails pass through mixed-hardwood forests, along rocky ridges, beside cascading waterfalls and past cultural features. Explore the Roomy Mine, an abandoned iron mine, in Norvin Green State Forest. A 360-degree vantage point at Wyanokie High Point presents a sweeping panorama of the nearby Wanaque Reservoir. Chikahoki Falls and the mixed-oak-hemlock ravine are equally beautiful. The Weis Ecology Center, run by the New Jersey Audubon Society, offers programs, workshops and other events. Wooded campsites and rustic cabins are available for rent by reservation only.

Wildlife to Watch

Start with bald eagle and osprey viewing over Wanaque Reservoir. The development of the reservoir system for New Jersey's cities has resulted in a tremendous increase in watershed protection and water quality improvement. It also created nesting and feeding habitat for osprey and eagles, as well as many other species of wildlife. These large birds of prey are proven indicators of environmental quality. Feeding largely on fish, their health reflects the quality of a food source shared by humans.

These forested ecosystems provide an excellent opportunity to see while-tailed deer, black bears, bobcats, red and gray foxes, striped skunks, Virginia opossums and many songbirds and raptors. In particular, look for the many kinds of warblers that breed and nest in the deep woods.

Trails

Take the 5.5-mile Blue Trail to Wyanokie High Point, a 900-foot cliff rising dramatically from the valley below. This challenging climb is well worth the effort. Often, there are red-tailed hawks or turkey vultures soaring above this point. Occasionally you may also spot a bald eagle or an osprey.

The 3.5-mile White Trail is a big loop-trail with easy-to-moderate terrain through mixed-hardwood forests to the most spectacular portion of the Chikahoki Falls. Look and listen for Louisiana and northern waterthrush, Blackburnian warbler and red-eyed vireo along the trail.

The challenging Yellow or Red trails (1 mile each over difficult terrain) go to the Roomy Mine, home to several species of bat as well as eastern pipistrelles. Do not enter the mine from November through April to avoid disturbing the hibernating bats. During the rest of the year, the best bat-viewing time is during midday, or at dusk when the bats leave to feed on insects in the nearby forest.

Trail maps are recommended and can be purchased at Weis Ecology Center or through the New York/New Jersey Trail Conference (www.nynjtc.org).

Site Notes	Norvin Green State Forest is open for hunting during prescribed seasons. Weis Ecology Center is only open Wednesday through Sunday. Closed Monday, Tuesday and holidays.
Size	Weis Ecology Center: 160 acres
	Norvin Green State Forest: 4,982 acres
Directions	From I-287, exit 55 in Wanaque, take CR 511 north for 3.8 miles to West Brook Road. The road is not marked from the south. Turn left (west) and travel for 2 miles on West Brook Road to Snake Den Road. Turn left (south) on Snake Den Road and go 0.7 mile, staying left at the fork to the Weis Ecology Center entrance.
Nearest Town	Ringwood
Ownership	Weis Ecology Center: New Jersey Audubon Society
	Norvin Green State Forest: NJDEP Division of Parks and Forestry
Contact	NJ Audubon Society: 973-835-2160; www.njaudubon.org
	Norvin Green State Forest: 973-962-7031; www.njparksandforests.org
Features	visitor center, interpretive programs, trails, hiking, restrooms, drinking water, picnicking

HIGHLANDS ■ Weis Ecology Center/Norvin Green State Forest

Great
▲ SITE ▲

Wildcat Ridge Wildlife Management Area

On a clear day the New York City skyline is visible

WIldcat Ridge hawk watch

PHOTO BY MIRIAM DUNNE/NJDFW

Description

Located in the Farny Highlands region, Wildcat Ridge and Split Rock Reservoir highlight this rugged landscape. Many trails lead over ridges to rocky overlooks, past wetlands and around crystal clear Split Rock Reservoir. The breathtaking view of the Highlands is well worth the hike to the top of the ridge. On a clear day the New York City skyline is visible, and the view provides an otherwise hard-to-obtain understanding of the vastness of the Highlands. No other area in north Jersey has the contiguous tracts of forest necessary to preserve healthy populations of endangered hawks, owls and rare songbirds.

Enjoy a hike or a paddle around scenic Split Rock Reservoir. The Hibernia Mine was once the state's largest known bat hibernaculum. Thousands of bats hibernated here until 2008, when the colony was devastated by White Nose Syndrome, a disease that has hit bat communities on the eastern seaboard.

Wildlife to Watch

Take the Overlook Trail to the top of the ridge to see migrating hawks. The fall migration is more spectacular, but either season offers great close-up views of raptors riding the thermals. In September, catch the spectacular broad-winged hawk migration. Red-tailed, sharp-shinned and Cooper's hawks, osprey, bald eagle and the occasional peregrine falcon peak in October. While raptors steal the show in fall, songbirds are the stars in spring.

The beaver-created wetlands are used by many species, including muskrat, otter and raccoon. Mallard, wood duck and American black duck also thrive in these small woodland wetlands, as do reptiles and amphibians. Beaver ponds provide

Great
▲ SITE ▲

critical habitat for eastern bluebirds and tree swallows, which nest in the cavities of dead and dying trees, and foraging areas for herons and belted kingfisher.

The disturbed, gravelly areas beyond the end of Upper Hibernia Road support interesting butterflies that use bluestem grasses, such as cobweb skipper, Indian skipper and dusted skipper. This same location is one of the best places in New Jersey for hoary edge skipper.

The best time to view bats is at dusk on spring or fall evenings. Bats swarm about the mine entrance in the evenings before moving off to hunt. Please do not approach the mine but observe the bats from the observation platform.

Audubon
IMPORTANT
BIRD AREAS

Trails

There are several miles of trails and most of them can be reached from one of the three parking areas. The trails are maintained by the New York/New Jersey Trail Conference and the Morris Trail Conservancy. Trail maps are available in the kiosk in the Split Rock Reservoir parking area.

Site Notes Wildcat Ridge is open for hunting during prescribed seasons.

Size 3,745 acres

Directions From I-80, take exit 37. Travel north on CR 513 toward Hibernia for 6.5 miles. Turn right on Upper Hibernia Road and proceed 2.6 miles to the parking area on the left to hike to the beaver pond. Stay on Upper Hibernia Road for 0.2 mile; this will lead you to parking and the trail to the hawk watch. For Splitrock Reservoir, turn onto Upper Hibernia Road then stay straight onto Split Rock Road. Cross the dam and park in the lot on the left.

Nearest Town Hibernia

Ownership NJDEP Division of Fish and Wildlife

Contact (973) 383-0918; www.njfishandwildlife.com

Features hiking, trails, restroom, parking, canoeing/kayaking, boat launch

Little Brown Bats   PHOTO BY NJDFW

Great
▲ SITE ▲

Black River Wildlife Management Area

Description

The Black River Valley forms a natural travelway for people as well as wildlife. The first settlers in northern New Jersey and Revolutionary War troops walked these pathways more than 200 years ago. Later, people and goods moved through this valley on horseback and by railroad. A rail-trail provides good opportunities to view freshwater and forested wetland and riparian habitat. The meandering river and its extensive freshwater marsh, next to upland forests and fields, contain a wide assortment of wildlife. Over 200 species of birds use the WMA and more than 100 nest here.

Wildlife to Watch

Spring and summer are the best times to visit but there is wildlife worth watching in all seasons. The muddy wetland edges are great places to look for the tracks of upland mammals and birds that visit the river. Deer come to drink, and mink and raccoons hunt for crayfish and turtle eggs at night. Belted kingfishers dive from perches at the water's edge to catch fish, and river otters ply for fish below the surface. Look for warblers, songbirds, wading birds, waterfowl, swallows and sandpipers in spring and summer. Waterfowl and raptors are easily seen in the fall and winter along with owls, woodpeckers and sparrows.

Trails

Patriot's Path runs for several miles along the rail-trail paralleling the river. Parking for the rail-trail is at the Pleasant Hill Road parking area.

Another good way to view wildlife in the Black River Valley is from the river itself. Launch a canoe upstream on Pleasant Hill Road and take a leisurely 3-mile paddle to the take-out point in the wildlife management area parking lot.

Site Notes: The Black River Wildlife Management Area is a natural area with no facilities. Open for hunting during prescribed seasons.

Size: 3,078 acres

Directions: Black River WMA: From US 206 in Chester, take CR 513 north for 2.8 miles to the WMA entrance on the left. Pleasant Hill Road: From US 206, take CR 513 north for 1 mile. At traffic light, turn left onto Oakdale Road. At the stop sign, turn right onto Pleasant Hill Road. Travel 0.2 mile to the parking area on the right before the river. The canoe take-out parking area is 0.2 mile past the railroad trail parking area on the left after you cross the river. To launch a canoe, travel 4.1 miles farther on Pleasant Hill Road. Parking lot and river access are on the right.

Nearest Town: Chester

Ownership: NJDEP Division of Fish, Game and Wildlife

Contact: 973-383-0918; www.njfishandwildlife.com

Features: parking, trails, hiking, biking, horseback riding

Fairview Farm Wildlife Preserve 24

Description

Fairview Farm is an Upper Raritan Watershed Association wildlife preserve. The watershed of the North Branch of the Raritan River and its tributaries comprises 194 square miles in Somerset, Hunterdon and Morris counties. The 170-acre preserve has an extensive trail system through old farm fields planted with native wildflowers and warm-season grasses, upland conifers and hardwoods, evergreen plantations and gardens, including a butterfly garden. The North American Butterfly Association identified 21 different species of butterflies during one field trip to the farm.

Wildlife to Watch

June is the nicest month here. It is cool, spring plants are blooming and there are 75 species of nesting birds to see. Watch for nesting grasshopper sparrows and bobolinks. Make the butterfly garden your first stop. Don't forget to watch for ruby-throated hummingbirds! Walk the trails through the fields and past the pond for a chance to see white-tailed deer, red fox, raccoon, eastern cottontail and red, gray and flying squirrels. Scan the pond for turtles, including the painted turtle, snapping turtle and the threatened wood turtle. Dragonflies are plentiful as well. Bird life abounds wherever you look.

Trails

Five miles of trails wind through fields and woods. Trails are open for hiking seven days a week from dawn to dusk. There is an informational kiosk in the parking area and trail maps are available online.

Site Notes: The office is open only on weekends. A composting toilet is located near the barn for times when the office is closed.

Size: 170 acres

Directions: From US 206 in Bedminster, take CR 512 west. Go 0.9 mile on CR 512 to Large Cross Road. Turn left and proceed for 0.5 mile to the farm's driveway on the right.

Nearest Town: Bedminster

Ownership: Upper Raritan Watershed Association

Contact: 908-234-1852; www.urwa.org

Features: hiking, trails, restroom

Musconetcong River Reservation/ Point Mountain Section 25

Description

Point Mountain, just south of the Musconetcong River, is part of the Musconetcong Mountain Range and one of the highest points in the region. It has a large expanse of maturing hardwood forest, fields, streams and geologic wonders. The name Point Mountain refers to the prominent pinnacle that sits at the top of this property.

Other sites

Wildlife to Watch

Take the Overlook Trail leading along the Musconetcong River and up to a lookout. The lookout is especially good in the fall for observing the small flights of hawks that occur in September and October. Some days up to 200 birds use the updraft from the ridges on their flights south. More than 70 species of birds breed on the site, including the forest-interior species—pileated woodpeckers, Acadian flycatchers and Kentucky and hooded warblers. May and June are the best birding months. Rare red-shouldered hawks and goshawks may also breed in this area.

Trails

There are five marked trails totaling three miles and ranging from moderate to difficult. Trail maps and information are available at http://www.co.hunterdon.nj.us/depts/parks/guides/PointMountain.htm#trails.

Site Notes: This is a natural area with no facilities.

Size: 700 acres

Directions: From NJ 31 in Hampton, take CR 645 north and east along the Musconetcong River for about 4 miles. Turn right onto Point Mountain Road. Park at the pullouts on either side of Point Mountain Road. Trailheads are near the bridge on Point Mountain Road and next to the Musconetcong River Reservation sign, near the junction of Point Mountain Road and CR 645.

Nearest Town: Hampton

Ownership: Hunterdon County Park System

Contact: 908-782-1158; www.co.hunterdon.nj.us/depts/parks/guides/PointMountain.htm#trails.

Features: trails, hiking, scenic overlook, horseback riding

Pohatcong-Alpha Grasslands Wildlife Management Area
26

Description

Originally destined for development, this important grassland bird habitat was saved by the Pohatcong Grasslands Association and is now managed specifically for grassland birds. Much of the land bordering this road is still being farmed but about 100 acres has been planted with warm season grasses. Drive the entire road slowly, scanning for birds, then pull off at the grasslands for a longer search.

Wildlife to Watch

This is a great winter birding spot and one of the most reliable spots in New Jersey to see snow buntings and lapland longspurs. Also, short-eared owls are common just before dusk and northern harriers and rough-legged hawks are frequent hunters during the day. Sparrows abound during all seasons. Look for tree, field, song, white-crowned, white-throated and Savannah sparrows in winter. Fox, Lincoln's, grasshopper, chipping and swamp sparrows are also present. Grasshopper sparrows breed here along with bobolink and eastern meadowlark. Vesper sparrows are uncommon but are sometimes spotted here.

Trails

This site doesn't have trails.

Site Notes: There is no defined parking area and through traffic is light on Oberly Road. Be aware of passing cars if you stop along the road. This is a natural area with no facilities. Please be respectful of the neighbors and do not trespass on adjacent private property.

Size: 128 acres

Directions: Take I-78 to exit 3. Follow signs to Alt. Route 22 toward Alpha. Take Alt. Route 22 east for 0.8 mile to CR 519. Take CR 519 south for 1.5 miles to CR 635. Turn right and go 1.3 miles to Oberly Road, first road on right. Travel 0.6 mile and pull onto the shoulder on the left.

Nearest Town: Alpha

Ownership: Phillipsburg Riverview Organization, NJDEP Division of Fish and Wildlife

Contact: 908-213-0101; http://proriverview.org

Features: no parking

Pyramid Mountain Natural Historical Area　　27

Description

Pyramid Mountain was established to protect this unique area, which is rich in natural and historical resources. The mountain provides diverse habitat for 400 species of native plants, more than 100 kinds of birds and 30 species of mammals. The area is best known for its unusual geologic formations such as Tripod Rock, a glacial erratic balanced on three small rocks. Lenape Indians flourished in the area as did early settlers; the result is a tapestry of fields, forests, streams and ponds.

Wildlife to Watch

Chestnut oaks and stands of beech trees provide forest cover for year-round residents like pileated woodpeckers, red-bellied woodpeckers, wild turkeys and black-capped chickadees. Summer neotropical visitors include scarlet tanagers, yellow warblers and indigo buntings. As you hike along the trails you may spot black bears, beavers, white-tailed deer, or coyotes. Bobcats still inhabit the region too. Cat Swamps and Cat Rocks areas were named for this shy forest inhabitant.

Trails

Five well-marked trails meander through and around fields, forests, rock outcroppings, streams and wetlands. The Blue Trail has an overlook with a view of New York City. Look for a famous glacial erratic named Tripod Rock. Trail maps are available at a kiosk in the parking area and online.

Site Notes: Park is open daily.

Size: More than 1,500 acres

Other sites

Directions: Take I-287 S to exit 45 (Myrtle Avenue in Boonton). Turn left onto Myrtle Avenue. Go to the second light. Turn right onto Wootton Street. Go up the hill to the 4-way stop. Turn right onto Boonton Avenue (County Road 511). After approximately 2.7 miles, turn left into Pyramid Mountain entrance.

Nearest Town: Boonton

Ownership: Morris County Park Commission

Contact: 973-334-3130; www.morrisparks.net

Features: trails, hiking, visitor center, restrooms, interpretive programs, drinking water and cross-country skiing

Saffin's Pond/Mahlon Dickerson Reservation — 28

Description

Saffin's Pond provides access to the larger Mahlon Dickerson Reservation, Morris County's largest park. Beechwoods, wetlands and grasslands surround the pond, one of many glacial lakes in the Berkshire Valley area.

Wildlife to Watch

Loop trails begin at the large parking lot. Walk around the pond, no more than a mile, through woods of tulip poplars, sassafras and rhododendrons. The glacial rocks and boulders deposited here more than 10,000 years ago are good perching places for listening to bullfrogs and songbirds in the spring. Breeding birds and beavers enliven walking trails in the summer. This is a great place to practice identifying ferns and violets.

Trails

There are over 20 miles of multi-use trails in the reservation, each with varying lengths and difficulty. Pine Swamp Trail leads to Headley Overlook, the highest point in Morris County (1,395 feet). Maps and information about trails and terrain are available online.

Site Notes: The park is open daily dawn to dusk

Size: Saffin's Pond: 1,000 acres; Mahlon Dickerson Reservation: 3,200 acres

Directions: From I-80, take exit 34B onto NJ 15 north. In Hurdtown, just over 4 miles on NJ 15, take the Weldon Road exit to the east. Continue on Weldon Road for 3.1 miles to the entrance on the right.

Nearest Town: Oak Ridge

Ownership: Morris County Park Commission

Contact: 973-326-7600; www.morrisparks.net

Features: biking, hiking, trails, camping, horseback riding, picnicking, cross-country skiing, restrooms, drinking water

Schiff Nature Preserve — 29

Description

The property contains typical habitats of the non-glaciated Highlands region, including hardwood successional forest, forested wetlands, stream corridors and riparian areas. The entire preserve is contained within the Ralston Historic District. Native American artifacts have been found along the rivers and streams. The Schiff Preserve provides a quiet, rugged haven in a busy community setting.

Wildlife to Watch

Hike to the 16-acre Great Meadow, a native warm-season grass restoration project, to see grassland birds, including eastern bluebird, American goldfinch and a variety of sparrows. Black-capped chickadee are easily seen and heard in the woodlands. Look for tracks of white-tailed deer and raccoon along the river. The wetlands attract a variety of frogs, snakes and turtles. Southern flying squirrels often reside in old woodpecker nest cavities.

Trails

Trails are open from dawn to dusk every day. Trail maps are located in a red informational kiosk. The preserve contains over 8 miles of trails which range in difficulty from easy to moderate. Trails are clearly marked. Please stay on the trails to minimize habitat destruction.

Site Notes: Check out the native plant garden with over 60 species of native plants. The nature center has no regular visitor hours. Call for event schedule or check online.

Size: 340 acres

Directions: Take exit 22B on I-287. Travel 3.5 miles on US 206 north. Turn right on Holland Road. Go to end and turn left onto Mosle Road. Go 2.7 miles and bear right onto Pleasant Valley Road. Go 0.1 mile and turn left into Schiff Natural Lands Trust. Go left at the "T" and travel 0.5 mile to parking area on top of ridge.

Nearest Town: Mendham

Ownership: Schiff Natural Lands Trust, Inc.

Contact: 973-543-6004; www.schiffnaturepreserve.org

Features: hiking, parking, interpretive center, picnicking, horseback riding, biking, restrooms, trails, observation platforms

South Branch Reservation/Echo Hill Environmental Education Area/Assiscong Marsh Natural Area   30

Description

The South Branch Reservation, almost 950 acres in size, was established to preserve the Raritan River and its environment. Evergreen bluffs, old farm fields and the Assiscong marsh, the largest marsh in Hunterdon County, are just some of its preserved areas. The Echo Hill Environmental Education Area has a lodge with a conference room and restrooms, the former Stanton Station railroad station, now an activity center, and camping or cabins for groups. Prescott Brook flows through the site, which also has large sycamores in a river-bottom forest, mature spruce and pine plantations, and a man-made pond.

Wildlife to Watch

A nature trail winds around the Echo Hill area, past the brook, through the evergreen forest and through a second-growth hardwood forest. The conifer

Other sites

stands here are among New Jersey's best and support nesting Cooper's hawk, red-breasted nuthatch and golden-crowned kinglet. Spring brings colorful wildflowers and migratory songbirds. In May and June look for wood turtle, eastern box turtle and snapping turtle. White-tailed deer may be encountered at any time. During the fall migration in September and October you are sure to see some fall warblers, as well as a few waterfowl. Raptors, owls and winter finches are part of the winter scene from November through March. Assiscong Marsh, located just a few miles away, is one of the best places to see all of New Jersey's dabbling ducks. There is also a good selection of divers, sandpipers, warblers and songbirds, depending on the season.

Trails

There are two miles of trails, which are easy walking except for ascending and descending the railroad embankment. Many of the trails are in the floodplain and can be muddy and slippery. Maps are available at the center or online at www.njtrails.org.

Site Notes: Limited hunting is allowed during some prescribed seasons. Hunters must obtain a permit from Hunterdon County Department of Parks and Recreation. Echo Hill is open during posted hours.

Size: 76 acres

Directions: Take NJ 31 south from I-78 for 5 miles. Turn right onto Stanton Station Road and continue for 0.4 mile. Turn right at Lilac Drive, just before the railroad and make a right turn at the entrance in another 0.4 mile. Assiscong Marsh: continue south on NJ 31 to CR 612 (Bartles Corner Road). Turn left and travel 0.6 mile to sharp left turn onto River Road (a dirt road). Go 0.2 mile to parking area on right.

Nearest Town: Clinton

Ownership: Hunterdon County Park System

Contact: 908-782-1158; www.co.hunterdon.nj.us

Features: trails, hiking, parking, camping

Spruce Run/Round Valley Recreation Areas   31

Description

The best time for viewing wildlife at these two sites is from fall through early spring. Both recreation areas have reservoirs that attract large numbers of waterfowl, wading birds, shorebirds, terns and even a few pelagic species on fall migration and during the winter. Spruce Run is next to Clinton Wildlife Management Area, which has more than 1,900 acres of field and woodlands. Spruce Run and Round Valley offer wilderness campsites for hikers and canoeists, that are available April 1 to October 31. Both have a variety of facilities and are very popular in the summer.

Wildlife to Watch

Winter waterbird watching is possible from many points around the reservoirs. The waterfowl most likely to be seen include mallards, American black ducks, canvasbacks, lesser scaup, ring-necked ducks, all three mergansers and Canada geese. Common and red-throated loon are usually seen in winter. Look for ruddy turnstones, greater and lesser yellowlegs, dunlins, short-billed dowitchers and solitary and spotted sandpipers in early fall. The peninsula by the boat launch at Spruce Run is the spot for gulls and terns.

Trails

There are three marked trails at Round Valley: the Cushetunk Trail, which accesses the campsites, the Pine Tree Trail and the Family Hiking and Biking Trail. All trails are accessed from the south parking lot within the day-use area. Stop in at the offices for maps and information.

A 0.9-mile section of the Highlands Millennium Trail runs through Spruce Run. This is an easy trail but not universally accessible.

Site Notes: Round Valley is open for hunting during prescribed seasons.

Size: Spruce Run: 2,012 acres; Round Valley: 3,684 acres

Directions: From Interstate 78, take exit 17 to NJ 31 north. Travel 3 miles to Van Syckel's Road. Turn left and travel 1.5 miles to the recreation area entrance on the left. For Round Valley, take I-78 to exit 18. Take US 22 east 2.3 miles to recreation area signs. Follow signs to boat ramp and office.

Nearest Town: Spruce Run: Clinton; Round Valley: Lebanon

Ownership: NJDEP Division of Parks and Forestry

Contact: Spruce Run: 908-638-8572; Round Valley: 908-236-6355; www.njparksandforests.org

Features: trails, camping, picnicking, restrooms, drinking water, boat launch, canoeing/kayaking, cross-country skiing, biking

Willowwood Arboretum/Bamboo Brook Outdoor Education Center   32

Description

Willowwood, named for a collection of 110 willows planted in the early twentieth century, has about 3,500 species of native and exotic plants. Plantings blend in with untouched wild areas. Meadows, fields and a forest on Western Hill border streams and the arboretum. Geologically, Willowwood is in the Piedmont region, while Bamboo Brook lies in the Highlands region. Both centers have eighteenth century houses and Bamboo Brook has a formal garden designed by Martha Brookes Hutcheson.

Wildlife to Watch

The trail through Long Meadow in Willowwood to Bamboo Brook gives you a chance to view many kinds of wildlife. Look for woodchucks, eastern bluebirds and American goldfinches feeding in the fields. Northern harriers and red-tailed hawks hunt for the small rodents you might not see. Multitudes of songbirds migrate in spring and fall and nest in the woods

Other sites

and wetland areas. Down by the brook look for wood frogs, southern leopard frogs and crayfish. Tracks of red foxes, raccoons, white-tailed deer and wild turkeys are more visible than the animals themselves.

Trails

Foot trails start from the parking areas of both centers. Pick up a map at the Myers Visitor Center at Willowwood Arboretum.

Site Notes: Open daily from dawn to dusk. The conservatory is open weekdays. Call for hours of operation.

Size: Willowwood Arboretum: 130 acres

Bamboo Brook Outdoor Education Center: 100 acres

Directions: From the junction of US 206 and CR 512, turn west onto CR 512 (Pottersville Road). Continue for 0.6 mile to Union Grove Road. Turn right and proceed 0.5 mile to Longview Road. Turn left on Longview Road. Entrances are 1 mile farther, on the left.

Nearest Town: Pottersville

Ownership: Morris County Park Commission

Contact: 973-326-7600; www.morrisparks.net

Features: visitor center, interpretive programs, trails, hiking, restrooms, drinking water

Monarch Butterfly *PHOTO BY JIM MALLMAN*

Northern Cardinal

Wood Turtle

Other sites

Metropolitan

★ Premier Sites
▲ Great Sites
● Other Sites

Ramsey
287
35
Pompton Lakes
42
37
Paterson
17
80 36 Hackensack
Clifton
23
Livingston
280
34 Union City
Madison Newark Jersey City
33
38
41
78 Elizabeth
94
1
22
40
287 39 95
Perth Amboy
New Brunswick

Urban wildlife viewing at its best

The name "Metropolitan" implies a heavily developed landscape and, in many respects, it accurately describes large portions of this region. However, as you explore the area, a different picture emerges. From the cliffs of the Palisades along the Hudson to the wetlands of the Hackensack Meadowlands and the gentle uplands of Union County, wildlife is everywhere.

As awareness of the importance of wildlife habitat has grown, the residents of the Metropolitan region have rallied to maintain and enhance their remaining wild areas. Parks and natural areas have been connected to form "greenways," where bike and walking paths allow people to enjoy the outdoors while viewing the wildlife that also rely on these travelways.

Bordered on the east by the Hudson River and Raritan Bay and on the west by the Highlands, the region contains a number of habitats, ranging from salty coves to upland forests. This diversity results in a vast array of wildlife—from harbor seals to the occasional black bear—and the area's wealth of bird life is simply extraordinary.

Although vast tracts of wetlands have been filled for development and land-fills, large areas of estuarine habitat remain. These areas, the Hackensack Meadowlands and Liberty State Park among them, are critical nurseries for marine and bird species. It surprises many to learn that sightings of snowy owls and peregrine falcons are not uncommon within sight of Manhattan. These and numerous other species have adapted to life in the region, and countless other bird species use the meadows and other natural areas as stepping stones in their biannual migrations. The riparian corridors, greenways and suburban parks also support a surprising variety of common mammals, such as raccoons, white-tailed deer, Virginia opossums, striped skunks, eastern cottontails, red fox and woodchucks, as well as diverse populations of reptiles, amphibians and breeding songbirds.

Common Merganser

PHOTO BY BOB CUNNINGHAM

Description

Located just 2,000 feet from the Statue of Liberty, Liberty State Park is a green oasis in the most densely populated region of New Jersey. Comprising 1,212 acres, the park includes wildlife habitats, open water, fields, nature trails, bike paths and a section of the Hudson River Waterfront Walkway, a spectacular waterfront promenade. Wildlife viewing is surprisingly good given the urban setting, but the combination of habitat and location along the Atlantic Flyway ensure that Liberty State Park is a haven for wildlife, particularly birds.

During the nineteenth and twentieth centuries, the area that is now Liberty State Park was a major waterfront industrial area and transportation hub. The restored Central Railroad of New Jersey Terminal was the starting point for millions of immigrants on their way to new lives. After being processed at nearby Ellis Island, immigrants would make their way to the terminal to begin a journey in their new country. As industry declined, the waterfront deteriorated and was eventually abandoned. The area was restored and opened on Flag Day in 1976 as New Jersey's bicentennial gift to the nation.

Many of the habitats within the park have been restored, and plans call for continued restoration on an additional 234 acres that was once a rail yard. Restoration will include salt marsh, fresh water wetlands, grasslands and successional northern hardwood and scrub-shrub forest. The 36-acre Richard J. Sullivan Natural Area lies adjacent to the interpretive center and contains one of the last remaining salt marshes in the Hudson River Estuary.

Liberty State Park is a great family destination. The history of the park and region is told in the Central Railroad of New Jersey Terminal. A ferry to Ellis Island and the Statue of Liberty leaves from the terminal. Taking a ferry ride

Premier
★ SITE ★

across the Hudson is a great way to see wildlife. The park's interpretive center, located on Freedom Way, provides a look at the natural history of the area, offers environmental education programs and keeps a "sightings" book. Liberty Science Center is rated one of the top ten must-see children's museums in the country.

Wildlife to Watch

With both estuarine and upland habitats, the park's bird list currently consists of 239 different species. Stroll along the Hudson River Waterfront Walkway year-round for great looks at ducks, grebes and loons and magnificent views of New York Harbor and the Manhattan skyline. Look for American black duck, gadwall, American wigeon (and occasionally a Eurasian wigeon), green-winged teal, American brant, ruddy duck, horned grebe, canvasback, bufflehead, and red-breasted, common and hooded mergansers. Common and least terns are frequently seen working the waters of the estuary in spring and summer. Don't discount the ubiquitous gulls. It is well worth scanning the flocks for the unusual find.

Woodland songbirds can be seen and heard along the nature path located in the upland portion of the Richard J. Sullivan Natural Area, while wading birds and shorebirds can be found in the salt marsh and adjacent tidal wetlands. Listen for the mellifluous burble of the marsh wren. Look for northern harrier hunting over the marsh all year and the occasional snowy owl in the winter. Walk out along the salt marsh at low tide when the exposed mud flats provide prime feeding and foraging habitat for black-crowned and yellow-crowned night herons in spring and summer. Snowy egrets, great egrets and great blue

Herring Gull

PHOTO BY BOB CUNNINGHAM

METROPOLITAN ■ Liberty State Park

herons stalk fish in the shallows, and diamondback terrapins pop their heads out of the water for air. Tree and barn swallows may be seen eating on the wing as they fly over the grassy fields. In the fall, migrating warblers make their way through the canopy along the nature path. Fall sparrows are plentiful and white-crowned and Lincoln's sparrow are frequently seen.

Trails

There are miles of accessible walkways through the park and along the waterfront that are suitable for walking and biking. There is a nature trail through Richard J. Sullivan Natural Area that makes for easy walking and wildlife watching. Contact the park for more information and a map of the park.

Site Notes	The park is open daily from 6 a.m. to 10 p.m. The interpretive center is usually open seven days a week from Memorial Day through Labor Day (closed most holidays). For more information, call 201-915-3409.
Size	1,212 acres
Directions	Liberty State Park is most easily accessed from the New Jersey Turnpike Extension, exit 14B. Immediately after tolls, turn left under the turnpike bridge to a traffic light. Go straight into the park. Go 1 mile and turn left onto Freedom Way. Travel to the interpretive center.
Nearest Town	Jersey City
Ownership	NJDEP Division of Parks and Forestry
Contact	interpretive center: 201-915-3409 general information: 201-915-3440 www.njparksandforests.org
Features	parking, restrooms, visitor center, interpretive center, picnicking, boat ramp, canoeing/kayaking, hiking, bicycling, interpretive programs, interpretive signage, food, drinking water

White-crowned Sparrow   *PHOTO BY STEVE BYLAND*

Premie ★ SITE

Snowy Egret

PHOTO BY STEVE BYLAND

Description

The NJMC Environment Center sits in the center of the 110-acre Richard W. DeKorte Park in the heart of the Meadowlands District, an area consisting of 14 municipalities. The center overlooks the Kingsland Tidal Impoundment, a tidal complex that attracts myriad types of wildlife. Named for the Hackensack River, the Hackensack Meadowlands is a vast tidal marsh encompassing 8,400 acres of now-vibrant fresh, brackish and salt marsh habitats. This is a stunning setting with an urban backdrop.

Prior to European settlement, the meadowlands consisted of several diverse marsh ecosystems surrounded by forests. Considered wasteland, for centuries the meadowlands underwent extraction of its natural resources, degradation of its water quality and filling of the wetlands for development and landfill sites. Much of the surrounding cities of Newark and Elizabeth were built on land that was drained and filled. Today there is a good deal of interest in the ecologic importance of the meadowlands, and significant areas have been preserved and restored to natural habitat.

Kingsland Overlook is a park on the edge of a landfill with views of a tidal marsh impoundment, backed by the dramatic New York City skyline. Five plant and wildlife communities have been established within this park: a wildflower meadow, butterfly meadow, eastern coastal grassland prairie, woody (shrub) field and a young woodland and evergreen forest. The adjoining Lyndhurst Nature Preserve is another landfill reclamation effort that turned an island of residential garbage into a lushly planted nature study area with spectacular views.

METROPOLITAN ■ New Jersey Meadowlands Commission Environment Center/Richard W. DeKorte Park

Premier
★ SITE ★

The environment center, operated by Ramapo College of New Jersey, boasts interactive exhibits about the ecology, history and restoration of the meadowlands, education programs for grades kindergarten through college and the public, and a view of the area that is unrivaled. Take time to visit the Jill Ann Ziemkiewicz Memorial Butterfly Garden, where many species of butterflies and other interesting insects come to nectar and lay their eggs from spring to fall.

Wildlife to Watch

The location of the Meadowlands along the Atlantic Flyway makes these urban marshlands vital to migratory fish and wildlife. More than 260 species of birds are attracted to the many habitats ranging from fresh and salt water wetlands to uplands. Each season has a predominant group of migrants. Residents include common moorhens, pied-billed grebes, ruddy ducks and gadwalls. Early spring brings the return of red-winged blackbirds and the air is alive with their raspy song. American robins are early returnees as well. Look for tree swallows to return in April and bobolinks in May, as well as indigo buntings and blue grosbeaks. Look for groundhogs feeding on new greenery.

A variety of shorebirds pass through from July through September. Check the mudflats in the Kingsland Tidal Impoundment for greater and lesser yellowlegs, short-billed dowitcher and least and semi-palmated sandpipers. Black skimmers feed in the shallows by gracefully skimming the water with their blade-like bills. Both yellow and black-crowned night heron breed here, as do snowy and great egrets and great blue herons. Look for ospreys fishing in the impoundment. Blue, mud and fiddler crabs, killifish and northern diamondback terrapins inhabit the marsh.

Fall and winter bring the raptor migration. Scan the marsh for northern harrier, American kestrel, red-tailed hawk, rough-legged hawk and short-eared and the occasional snowy owl. The gull watching is good here, with an occasional sighting of an Iceland or glaucous gull. Fall waterfowl include American black ducks, common and hooded mergansers, northern shovelers, canvasbacks, green-winged teal, northern pintail and bufflehead. Many species of waterfowl can be seen in winter unless the impoundment freezes over.

Audubon
IMPORTANT
BIRD AREAS

Trails

There are eight miles of walking trails in the Meadowlands District, incorporating low-impact construction, native plantings and recycled materials. Most of the paths originate in DeKorte Park and are universally accessible. The Marsh Discovery Trail is part of a 0.5-mile loop on a floating boardwalk around Kingsland Tidal Impoundment. Trail guides are available in the center or in boxes on bulletin boards near the parking lots. The Sawmill Creek Trail leads

METROPOLITAN ■ New Jersey Meadowlands Commission Environment Center/Richard W. DeKorte Park

Premier
★ SITE ★

to the vast mudflats within Sawmill Creek Wildlife Management Area. There are also two marked canoe/kayak trails, Mill Creek Marsh and Sawmill Creek.

Site Notes The trails are open daily from dawn to dusk. The Environment Center is open Monday-Friday 9 a.m.-5 p.m., weekends 10 a.m.-3 p.m. Closed holidays. Maps of the canoe/kayak trails and walking trails are available at the center.

Size 19,730 acres (entire district)

Directions From the New Jersey Turnpike, exit 16W, take NJ 3 west to NJ 17 south (Lyndhurst exit). Follow the ramp onto Polito Avenue and continue to the end of Polito Avenue. At the stop sign, turn left onto Valley Brook Avenue and continue 1.5 miles to its end. Continue straight across the railroad tracks to the environment center on the left.

Nearest Town Lyndhurst

Ownership New Jersey Meadowlands Commission

Contact 201-460-8300; www.njmeadowlands.gov

Features parking, restrooms (in center), picnicking, hiking, trails, visitor center, interpretive programs, interpretive signage, scenic overlooks, observation platforms/blinds, drinking water, canoeing/kayaking

Killdeer

PHOTO BY BOB CUNNINGHAM

Premier
★ SITE ★

Northern Shoveler

PHOTO BY BOB CUNNINGHAM

Description

Once truly a celery farm, this site is a delightful treasure set amidst suburban sprawl. This small jewel contains a freshwater cattail marsh, overgrown fields, a hardwood swamp, a small copse of woods and a 20-acre lake. Birders report that 240 species of birds use this area throughout the year. Once drained, the farm's elevated water levels now create several acres of flooded marsh. Dramatic numbers of nesting and migratory birds arrive in spring and fall. Volunteers maintain an active nest box program for several species of cavity nesters.

Wildlife to Watch

Spring is the time to look for the elusive American bittern, state-threatened long-eared owl and state-endangered red-shouldered hawk. Take a break on the observation platform to enjoy viewing and listening to red-winged blackbird, yellow warbler, great egret, double-crested cormorant, Canada geese, green heron, willow flycatcher, Virginia rail, common moorhen, marsh wren and sora in spring or summer. Most of the common wading birds can be seen stalking fish and frogs. Look for green frogs and bullfrogs and painted and snapping turtles. You might even glimpse an eastern cottontail or white-tailed deer while quietly strolling the path. A huge array of waterfowl depend upon Celery Farm during fall migration, with visitors including both divers and dabblers. There are also huge mixed flocks of swallows and hundreds of bobolinks. A variety of sparrows flit from perch to ground in the overgrown fields looking for berries and seeds. Look for American tree, song, swamp, savannah and white-throated sparrows and dark-eyed junco.

Trails

Steal two hours from the day and take an easy, leisurely walk along the 1.3-mile footpath around Lake Appert to look for wildlife.

Site Notes	Parking is limited to 10 cars.
Size	97 acres
Directions	Take Garden State Parkway exit 165 and drive west on Ridgewood Avenue. Travel 0.8 mile to New Jersey 17 north. Travel north for 5.3 miles to the exit for Allendale. Follow East Allendale Avenue west for 1 mile to Franklin Turnpike. Turn right and go 0.3 mile to parking lot on right.
Nearest Town	Allendale
Ownership	Allendale Borough
Contact	201-327-3470; www.fykenature.org
Features	observation platform, trails, hiking

Red-winged Blackbird

PHOTO BY JIM MALLMAN

Great
▲ SITE ▲

White-eyed Vireo

PHOTO BY STEVE BYLAND

Description

These parks provide an oasis of green in a sea of development. This, coupled with their ridgetop location at the end of the first Watchung Mountain, guarantees a panoply of songbirds during spring migration. Located just 15 miles west of the Hudson River, Garret Mountain offers outstanding vistas of the Newark Basin and New York City. Most of the park's landscape is upland mixed-hardwood forest, primarily oak-hickory. Three small brooks provide important riparian habitat. Garret Mountain has been designated as one of only 12 National Natural Landmarks in New Jersey by the National Park Service for its exceptional biological and geological features. It is one of the best places to view the spring songbird migration.

Wildlife to Watch

Hit the trail around Barbour's Pond for swallows, sandpipers and wood warblers. Look for both Baltimore and orchard orioles as well as scarlet and summer tanagers. See if you can hear or see five species of woodpeckers: downy, hairy, red-bellied, pileated and northern flicker. Many species of sparrows overlap here in May. Chipping, swamp and song sparrows are arriving while dark-eyed junco, white-throated and white-crowned sparrows are leaving. White-breasted nuthatches are ubiquitous. Take time to scour the woods inside the loop road for thrushes. Even gray-cheeked, Swainson's and Bicknell's can be common here—Bicknell's rarely. Warbler species can include mourning, orange-crowned, prothonotary, Kentucky and yellow-breasted chat. All the vireos except Philadelphia have been seen and Olive-sided flycatchers often reside here.

METROPOLITAN ■ Garret Mountain/Rifle Camp Park

Great ▲ SITE ▲

94

Trails

There are many marked trails of varying lengths and difficulties in both parks. Some trails are paved and most allow multi-use for hiking, running, cross-country skiing and horseback riding.

Site Notes Birds stay active here well into the day. Both parks have a deep and varied history with many historic sites located within park boundaries. Rifle Camp Park has a nature center and observatory. Call 973-523-0024 for events.

Size Garrett Mountain Reservation: 568 acres

Rifle Camp Park: 160 acres

Directions Garret Mountain Reservation: Take exit 56A on I-80 onto Squirrelwood Road. Go 0.4 mile and bear right onto Rifle Camp Road. In 0.2 mile, make a hard left onto Mountain Avenue. Look for park entrance on the right in 0.2 mile.

Rifle Camp Park: Follow directions above onto Rifle Camp Road. Continue on Rifle Camp Road for 0.9 mile to park entrance on the left. Drive to end of park road and park at the nature center.

Nearest Town West Patterson

Ownership County of Passaic

Contact 973-881-4832; www.passaiccountynj.org/ParksHistorical/Parks/garretmountainreservation.htm

Features restrooms, trails, drinking water, interpretive center, hiking, horse-back riding, cross-country skiing, observation blind, picnicking

Gray-Cheeked Thrush   *PHOTO BY BOB CUNNINGHAM*

Great
▲ SITE ▲

Palisades Interstate Park   PHOTO BY ANTHONY TARANTO, COURTESY PALISADES INTERSTATE PARK COMMISSION

Description

The 190-million-year-old Palisades tower above the Hudson River and are the best remaining examples of thick diabase in the United States. The cliffs were formed when magma from beneath the surface of the earth was forced upward between layers of sandstone and shale, making what is known as diabase. The diabase, or trap rock, was quarried extensively in the last century. Palisades Interstate Park and the Park Commission were formed in 1900 to protect the Palisades from further destruction.

The New Jersey section of the park encompasses 2,500 acres of wild Hudson shoreline, miles of upland forests and the cliffs themselves. There are 30 miles of hiking trails, two public boat basins, four picnic areas and three scenic overlooks located along Palisades Parkway. The Palisades are a National Natural Landmark and the park itself is a National Historic Landmark. Two nationally recognized trails, the Long Path and the Shoreline Trail, run the length of the New Jersey section.

Wildlife to Watch

Take the hiking trail from the parking area at Alpine Boat Basin to look for evidence of the last remaining eastern woodrat population in New Jersey. A native species, the woodrat is less aggressive than competing exotic rat species. Scan the Hudson for winter waterfowl including Barrow's goldeneye, bufflehead, canvasback and common loon. Wintering bald eagles are plentiful. The

Great
▲ SITE ▲

Palisades provide rare natural cliff habitat for peregrine falcon, and up to four pair of these magnificent birds nest here annually. View the fall migration of raptors from either the Alpine Boat Basin or State Line Lookout. Hiking the trails is a good way to experience the spring songbird migration. The Hudson River is a major spawning ground for shad, striped bass and sturgeon. This is also one of the most reliable places to see the uncommon pipevine swallowtail butterfly. Look for them draped on sunlit vegetation along the cliffs.

Audubon
IMPORTANT
BIRD AREAS

Trails

The shore trail begins at the southern park entrance where it descends to run along the Hudson. It steeply ascends at its end just north of the New York state line. The Long Path runs along the cliff top and its terrain is easy to moderate. There are several shorter trails that vary in length and terrain from 0.5 mile to 3 miles and moderate to steep. There are six cross-country ski trails that can be used by hikers as well. Go to www.njpalisades.org/longpath.htm for a mile-by-mile description of the Long Path.

Site Notes Trails are open seven days a week during daylight hours.

Size 2,500 acres

Directions From I-95 EXPRESS LANES: Take exit 73 (last exit in New Jersey). Turn right at the light onto Bruce Reynolds Boulevard. Turn right at light onto Lemoine Avenue. Entrance to the park is 0.5 mile ahead on right.

Nearest Town Alpine

Ownership Palisades Interstate Park Commission

Contact 201-768-1360; www.njpalisades.org

Features boat launch, canoe/kayak, hiking, trails, picnicking, restrooms, drinking water, scenic overlook

Northern Goshawk PHOTO BY STEVE BYLAND

METROPOLITAN ■ Palisades Interstate Park

Great
▲ SITE ▲

Trailside Nature and Science Center/ Watchung Reservation

Butterfly garden provides up-close encounters with wildlife

Least Sandpiper   PHOTO BY BOB CUNNINGHAM

Description

Trailside Nature and Science Center sits in the center of the Watchung Reservation, Union County's largest park. Located in a wooded preserve between the first and second ridges of the Watchung Mountains, this site is a great place to experience the spring songbird migration. Trailside hosts New Jersey's first natural history museum, built in 1941. Facilities include the visitor center, exhibits, museum and a planetarium. The site is mostly wooded and the Civilian Conservation Corps planted a pine plantation here in the 1930s that has grown into a mature forest. A butterfly garden and backyard habitat demonstration areas are good places to see wildlife up close.

Wildlife to Watch

White-tailed deer and gray squirrels are abundant and can frequently be seen from the trails in the woods. Great horned owls nest in the conifers and can often be heard hooting near dusk. Watch for pileated woodpeckers as well. Look for ovenbird, Louisiana waterthrush and eastern phoebe as you walk along Blue Brook. Prothonotary, Kentucky and worm-eating warblers are known to breed here on occasion. Several species of sparrows and eastern bluebirds frequent the scout camping area, and belted kingfishers, Baltimore orioles and a variety of migrating shorebirds can be seen at Little Seely's Pond.

Trails

More than 13 miles of hiking trails traverse wooded hillsides and scenic ridgetops. Several different trails lead around Lake Surprise and along Blue Brook. The trails

Great
▲ SITE ▲

are of varying length from 0.5 mile to 10 miles and range in difficulty from easy to moderate. While most of the trails aren't universally accessible, visitors can drive to some of the viewing areas. Trail maps are available at the center or online.

Site Notes The visitor center is open daily in the afternoon.

Size 1,945 acres

Directions From westbound I-78 take exit 43. Turn right at first traffic light onto McMane Avenue. Follow to the "T" intersection with Glenside Avenue and turn left. Go 1.2 miles and turn right onto CR 645 (Tracy Drive) and enter the reservation. Pass Surprise Lake and continue on Tracy Drive to the traffic circle. Take the first right onto Summit Lane. Go 0.5 mile and turn right onto New Providence Road. Follow signs to the science center in 0.25 mile.

Nearest Town Mountainside

Ownership Union County Division of Parks and Recreation

Contact 908-89-3670; www.ucnj.org/trailside

Features visitor center, interpretive programs, trails, hiking, restrooms, drinking water, horseback riding, picnicking

Northern Water Snake

Gr
▲ SI
9

Dismal Swamp 39

Description

Dismal Swamp is one of the last remaining wetlands in a highly urbanized environment. It is designated a priority wetland by the U.S. Fish and Wildlife Service and EPA. The area features wetlands that are of unique ecological value and support a diverse and important number of wildlife, including 165 species of birds. The upland deciduous forest contains mature trees, and an abandoned field adds richness. The swamp provides important ecological services for nearby communities by filtering water and providing floodwater storage for adjacent Bound Brook.

Wildlife to Watch

The swamp supports a variety of wildlife. Look for green herons, American bitterns, American black ducks, northern harriers, Virginia rails, spotted sandpipers, yellow-billed cuckoos and eastern phoebes in the wetlands and fields. Songbirds are numerous in the wetland and upland forests, and endangered loggerhead shrikes are reported to breed here. Sightings of endangered grasshopper sparrows are also on record. The swamp's mammals include white-tailed deer, raccoons and eastern cottontails. Northern water snakes are among the reptiles present.

Trails

Take the Dismal Swamp Trail from Metuchen for a short but interesting hike through a portion of the swamp. The trail is fun for children and unique in that it uses fallen trees as observation blinds and bridges.

Site Notes: Parking is limited and there are no facilities.

Size: 650 acres

Directions: From New Jersey 27 in Metuchen, turn north onto Central Avenue and go left (west) to Liberty Street. Proceed for 0.6 mile to a cul-de-sac. The entrance to the observation trail is located near the kiosk.

Nearest Town: Metuchen

Ownership: Edison Township, Borough of Metuchen

Contact: 908-632-8520; www.metuchennj.org/dismal_swamp.html

Features: parking, trail

Highland Avenue Woods Reserve 40

Description

This tiny preserve, just 36 acres, is packed with plants and animals. Situated between industrial and residential development, this area's fertile soils once supported agriculture and logging. Visitors can explore streams, woods and fields. Spring wildflowers are abundant in the woods. Habitats include a mix of upland and wetland communities that provide breeding, resting and feeding areas for a variety of wildlife.

es

Wildlife to Watch

Birders have logged 75 species of birds over the course of a year. Look for red-tailed hawk, ruby-throated hummingbird, black-crowned night heron and wood thrush in the spring and summer. Black-throated green warbler, warbling vireo and yellow-rumped warbler are seen in spring. Red-backed salamander, spring peeper and wood frog are among the denizens of the wetlands. Mammals are present but often elusive. Look for raccoon, muskrat, gray squirrel, northern flying squirrel, eastern cottontail, red, little brown and big brown bats and beaver. A variety of butterflies enjoy the flowering plants in the reserve.

Trails

There are several trails winding through the preserve. The terrain is fairly level but the surface can be rough. Trails are open from dawn to dusk seven days a week.

Site Notes: The South Plainfield Environmental Specialist is available at Borough Hall, 2480 Plainfield Avenue Monday through Friday.

Size: Approximately 25 acres

Directions: From Interstate 287, take the Edison exit from the north or the Durham Avenue exit from the south. From Durham Avenue, turn left onto Hamilton Boulevard, then right onto South Clinton Avenue, then right onto Sylvania Place. From the Edison exit, turn left onto Stelton Avenue, then right onto Hamilton Boulevard and proceed as above.

Nearest Town: South Plainfield

Ownership: Borough of South Plainfield

Contact: 908-226-9000; http://www.geocities.com/friendsofhighlandwoods/

Features: nature center, interpretive programs, trails, hiking, restrooms, interpretive signs

Lenape Park

Description

Located in an urban setting, Lenape Park is on the floodplain of the north branch of the Rahway River and includes the Nomahegan and Black Brook tributaries. Present habitats include hardwood forest, floodplain forests, grassy fields and forested wetlands. There is a pond at the park's west end that provides a resting and feeding area for migratory birds. Lenape Park is part of a green chain of parks protecting the Rahway River and providing a riparian corridor for wildlife. Earthen berms parallel the river in the park and provide excellent viewing opportunities for visitors, as well as flood control for local towns.

Wildlife to Watch

There are good viewing opportunities in the parking lot, and an easy 1.5-mile walk on a trail brings countless possibilities. More than 100 species of birds have been seen here along with white-tailed deer, gray squirrels and a good variety of turtles. Spring migration brings yellow, Nashville, Canada, blackpoll, northern parula and Wilson's warblers. Look and listen for bullfrogs, green frogs and northern gray treefrogs. Summer nesting species include orchard and northern orioles, eastern wood-pewees, willow flycatchers, American redstarts and ruby-throated hummingbirds. Fall migration heralds the arrival of sharp-shinned, broad-winged and red-shouldered hawks, pied-billed grebes, common nighthawks and several bat species. Occasional visits by such birds as peregrine falcons, hooded mergansers and bobolinks keep bird watching interesting for all birders.

Trails

There is an easy-to-walk 1.5-mile trail.

Site Notes: Lenape Park is a natural area with few facilities.

Size: 450 acres

Directions: From US Highway 22 in Cranford, turn onto County Route 577 south which becomes County Route 509 east within 1 mile. Continue on CR 509 east for a short distance; the parking area is on your left. (The total distance from US 22 is less than 1 mile.)

Nearest Town: Cranford

Ownership: Union County Department of Parks and Recreation

Contact: 908-527-4900; www.ucnj.org/parks

Features: parking

Tenafly Nature Center   42

Description

Tenafly Nature Center is a small gem tucked away in a busy suburban landscape. The diversity of habitats includes a buttonbush swamp, streams and a 3-acre pond brimming with wildlife. The deciduous forest contains mixed-oak species, sugar maple, black birch and a rich understory of spring wildflowers. Don't miss the backyard habitat demonstration area. Visitors delight in the eastern chipmunks that scurry around the interpretive center.

Wildlife to Watch

Frogs and turtles are common in the spring and summer at Pfister's Pond, about 600 feet from the parking area on the main trail. Sunfish may be seen nesting in the pond at the trail's edge. Breeding birds using the pond include wood duck, green heron, black-crowned night heron and belted kingfishers. Songbird viewing is excellent along the trails along the buttonbush swamp and through the woods in spring and fall.

Trails

There are seven miles of trails to hike at Tenafly that vary in length and terrain, but most are relatively easy. The trails are open every day from dawn to dusk. Trail maps are available online or at the visitor center.

Site Notes: The visitor center is open seven days a week.

Size: 400 acres

Directions: From US Highway 9W, take East Clinton Avenue 1.9 miles west to Engle Street. Turn right and travel 0.7 mile to Hudson Avenue. Turn right again and follow Hudson Avenue to its terminus.

Nearest Town: Tenafly

Ownership: Borough of Tenafly, managed by Tenafly Nature Center Association

Contact: 201-568-6093; www.tenaflynaturecenter.org

Features: visitor center, interpretive programs, trails, hiking, cross-country skiing

Piedmont

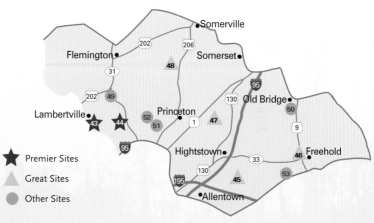

Somerville

202   206

Flemington•   Somerset•
31   48

202   49
Lambertville•   Princeton   130 Old Bridge•
43   44   52   •   47   50
51   1   9

★ Premier Sites   95   Hightstown•   33   46 Freehold•

▲ Great Sites   130   53
195   45

● Other Sites   •Allentown

Gently rolling farmlands and winding river valleys

The Piedmont Region is part of the Triassic Lowland physiographic province extending from the Blue Ridge Mountains in the south to Connecticut in the north. The landscape of this region is gently rolling lowland bisected by broad, winding river valleys with well-developed floodplains. The gentle contours of the countryside are interrupted by a number of distinctly higher rocky ridges and hills, including the Hunterdon Plateau and Sourland Mountain. These landforms were created during the breakup of the Pangean "supercontinent" approximately 200 million years ago as rift valleys formed, filled, eroded, tilted, uplifted, became injected with magma and eroded further. Today the land continues to be shaped through weathering and erosion.

Although the heavily developed U.S. Route 1 corridor bisects this region, it is still dominated largely by farm fields, pastures, woodlands, swamps and rocky ridges. Fortunately, many acres within this area are preserved as public open space. The Hunterdon County Park System, Washington Crossing State Park, Assunpink Wildlife Management Area, Delaware & Raritan Canal State Park and the Stony Brook-Millstone Watershed Association are some of the public lands that offer high-quality wildlife viewing opportunities.

In early spring the forest floor is lined with lycopodium and skunk cabbage. As spring progresses May apples, violets, jack-in-the-pulpits, wild azaleas, sweetgum, hickory, tulip-poplar, black cherry and beech trees bloom. Greenbriar, Virginia creeper, poison ivy and wild grape creep over the underbrush. In the wooded bogs and swamps of the region, red maple, black gum, ash and birch are the dominant trees, while blueberry, sweet pepperbush and buttonbush grow in the understory. Sphagnum moss, swamp rose and blue flag iris provide a herbaceous layer.

Woodpeckers, blue jays, northern cardinals, tufted titmice and chickadees are glimpsed here year-round. During spring and fall the forest is abuzz with the songs of migrant birds. In winter, mink tracks are a common sight along the banks of streams. Listen and look for several species of amphibians, especially during the spring breeding season. Eastern chipmunks, gray squirrels and white-tailed deer are the most commonly seen mammals. Look for waterfowl, particularly wood ducks, in rivers and streams.

Field Sparrow

Although it is disappearing at an alarming rate, this region still supports areas of agricultural land. Both hay fields and fields lying fallow are important because they provide prime habitat for endangered grassland birds, including upland sandpipers, vesper sparrows, grasshopper sparrows and bobolinks as well as mammals like coyotes, white-tailed deer and eastern cottontail rabbits. Watch for red-tailed hawks and American kestrels hunting over open fields or perching in trees or on telephone wires. Wild turkeys also frequent open fields and meadows.

Ground-nesting killdeer feed in open areas, while swallows feed on insects overhead. In the fall thousands of Canada geese feed on cut grain, and sand-pipers, dowitchers and yellowlegs frequent puddles after autumn rains. Field edges contain a mix of native and ornamental shrubs and understory trees such as sassafras, dogwood, Russian olive, multiflora rose and blackberry brambles, which provide food and cover for wildlife. Edge habitats are particularly attractive to northern mockingbirds, woodchucks, bobwhite quail and ring-necked pheasants.

At higher elevations the vegetation reflects the drier habitat and thinner soil. Oak-hickory forests are bursting with grasses, forbs, mosses and lichens found growing on exposed south and west facing slopes. Toads, eastern box turtles, eastern chipmunks, gray squirrels, songbirds and white-tailed deer are the main inhabitants of this dry, less-diverse habitat.

The Piedmont is characterized by low, rolling hills and well-drained, fertile soil. Farm fields, especially those not in crop rotation, provide important habitat for edge-dwelling species. Many animals visit fields at different times of the day or year to meet a variety of needs. Fields are generally very different from surrounding habitats. They heat more quickly than other areas due to their constant exposure to sunlight.

White-tailed deer come to fields to browse on fresh green shoots in the spring. Hibernators like woodchucks and snakes come out to bask in the sun. Flowering plants draw insects which attract birds and later produce seeds which are eaten by birds and rodents. The loose soil attracts burrowers like toads and meadow voles which, in turn, attract red foxes, hawks and owls. Fields also provide cover for ground-nesting birds and small mammals, including eastern cottontails.

Eastern Cottontail   PHOTO BY JIM MALLMAN

River Jewelwing

PHOTO BY JOHN PARKE

Description

Once the towpath (a path parallel to a canal allowing vehicles or animals to tow a vessel up the canal) for the historic Delaware & Raritan Canal, this 70-mile linear park is one of New Jersey's most popular recreational corridors and part of the National Recreational Trail System. Thirty-six of the 44 miles of the main canal, stretching from Trenton to New Brunswick, and all 22 miles of the feeder canal, Trenton to Frenchtown, still exist, providing miles of accessible multi-use trails. Many of the original historic structures also remain. The canals wind through quaint communities, farmland and forests, providing an important habitat connection for wildlife. There are numerous points of access, and birding is good all along the canals, especially in the spring. Fall migration is good, but birds are harder to see because of the leaves on the trees. Surveys within the park identified 160 species of birds and 90 of those nest here. Many of the historic sites are open for visitation throughout the year. Stop at the park office or visit the website prior to your visit for maps and information.

Two renowned spots for wildlife watching in the park are Bull's Island Recreation Area and Six Mile Run Reservoir Site. Bull's Island was created when the canal was dug and a narrow spit of land was separated from the mainland by the canal. It is considered one of the best examples of riparian habitat along the Delaware and is known by birders as one of the few places in New Jersey to see nesting northern parula and cerulean warblers. It also hosts Acadian flycatchers, cliff swallows and Louisiana waterthrushes. The best time to visit here is April through June for the songbird migration. The pedestrian bridge over

PIEDMONT ■ Delaware & Raritan Canal State Park

Premier
★ SITE ★

the Delaware River provides birders with a rare opportunity to look directly into the trees bordering the river. This is also a great, very scenic place from which to scan the river. You can frequently see five species of swallows from the bridge. The northern end of the island holds the park's campsite and, in spite of the activity, is a good and accessible place to bird in spring and summer. Walk the trail through the natural area on the southern end to experience a lowland floodplain forest dominated by sycamore, silver maple and tulip poplar, but beware of stinging nettle. Several rare plant species are found here.

Once slated to become a reservoir, the Six Mile Run Reservoir Site still reflects its agricultural history. Settled by Dutch immigrants in the 1700s, many of the original farmhouses and barns still exist. The Six Mile Run Historic District is included in the National Register of Historic Places. Much of the 3,000-acre site is still farmed by local farmers who lease the land. The remaining land is deciduous forest, fallow fields and riparian floodplain. This refuge amidst ever-expanding development provides important habitat for both resident and migratory wildlife.

Wildlife to Watch

The many fallow fields throughout the park make the area attractive to American kestrel. The fields are also used by American woodcock, northern bobwhite, field, grasshopper and song sparrows, American goldfinch, eastern meadowlarks and blue grosbeaks. Take one of the trails through the woods along Six Mile Run and listen and look for blue-gray gnatcatchers, white-eyed vireos, eastern towhee and scarlet tanagers. There is a bald eagle nest nearby and red-tailed hawks breed here as well. Be on the lookout for eastern box turtles, American toads and leopard frogs. Look for little brown bats at dusk or possibly a red or gray fox making its way back to its den at first light. Walk the towpath and scan the Delaware River for waterfowl in winter and sandpipers in spring and fall. Great blue and green herons feed from the banks of the canal and wood ducks dabble along the edges. Listen for the dry rattle of the belted kingfisher or the slap of a beaver's tail. Red-bellied and painted turtles and red-eared sliders sun themselves on fallen logs or along the bank. Don't miss the shad migration in the Delaware from late March to late May.

Trails

There are more than 70 miles of trails in the park, and most of the towpath along the canals is universally accessible. There is a 1.0-mile, easy loop trail through the natural area at Bull's Island. Six Mile Run Reservoir Site has several marked trails of varying lengths, the longest being the blue trail at 3.8 miles. Trail users can combine the red and blue trails for a 5.3-mile hike. The elevation difference is minimal making for easy walking but trail sections in the floodplain can be muddy at times. Horseback riding is permitted on all but the yellow trail.

Site Notes Maps and event information are available at park offices or online at www.dandrcanal.com. Canoes can be rented at Griggstown and Princeton access areas. Parking areas are located along the length of the park.

Size 5,379 acres

Directions Main park office: From Princeton, take US 1 north to exit for CR 522 (Ridge Road). Turn left at bottom of ramp heading towards the town of Kingston. Go approximately 1 mile. Turn left onto Division Street. At the stop sign turn left onto Academy Street, which becomes Mapleton Road. The park office and Mapleton Preserve is located 0.2 mile on the left.

Bull's Island Recreation Area: From Stockton, take NJ 29 north for 3.5 miles to marked entrance on the left.

Six Mile Run Reservoir Site: From Princeton, take US 206 north for approximately 3 miles. Turn right onto CR 518. Go 1 mile and turn left onto CR 632 (Canal Road). Follow CR 632 for approximately 4.5 miles to park office on right (625 Canal Road).

Nearest Town Princeton

Ownership NJDEP Division of Parks and Forestry

Contact 609-924-5705; www.njparksandforests.org

Features parking, hiking, biking, horseback riding, trails, camping, canoeing/ kayaking, picnicking, restrooms, drinking water, visitor center/office

Blue-gray Gnatcatcher

PHOTO BY STEVE BYLAND

Premier ★ SITE ★

PIEDMONT ▪ *Delaware & Raritan Canal State Park*

Red-breasted Nuthatch

PHOTO BY BOB CUNNINGHAM

Description

Washington Crossing State Park is situated just 8 miles north of Trenton and is the site of General Washington's renowned crossing of the Delaware on Christmas night in 1776 on his way to the Battle of Trenton. The park, appearing much as it might have in 1776, is a great place to see wildlife. Start at the visitor center for a history lesson and to pick up a map. The habitats of the park are varied and include old fields, deciduous forest, pine plantations, a natural area and a stream corridor.

The Ted Stiles Preserve is sandwiched between Washington Crossing State Park to the south and the Howell Living History Museum to the north in a bucolic country setting. Baldpate Mountain, part of the Sourland range, presumably got its name in the mid-1900s when its top was cleared for a landing strip. The visitor center is located in an old estate home called "Strawberry Hill" and presents a spectacular view west and south over the Delaware River and into Pennsylvania. The preserve is named for Rutgers University professor Ted Stiles, who was instrumental in its preservation.

When visiting Washington Crossing State Park, start in the lawns and gardens around the center. Look for northern cardinal, blue jay, American robin and northern mockingbird. Walk along Continental Lane toward the river in winter to see red-breasted nuthatches, brown creeper and golden-crowned kinglets. You can often see white-tailed deer or groundhogs in the fields along the lane even during the day. Scan the Delaware for fish crows, gulls, common and hooded mergansers, common goldeneye and bufflehead in winter and watch

PIEDMONT ■ *Washington Crossing State Park/Ted Stiles Preserve at Baldpate Mountain*

Premier
★ SITE ★

the banks for sandpipers in spring and fall. In summer cliff swallows occasionally nest under the bridge and tree and barn swallows feed on insects over the river. Check the sky for turkey and black vultures in most seasons. Check the ground for two-lined, redback and northern dusky salamanders, pickerel frogs and American toads. Go on an evening owl prowl to listen for eastern screech and great horned owls.

Take a walk on the trails in spring for red-eyed and white-eyed vireos, blue-winged, prairie and yellow warblers, American redstart, brown thrasher and rose-breasted grosbeak. The nature center offers regular events. Call 609-737-0609 or go to www.nj.gov/dep/parksandforests/parks/washington_crossing_calendar.htm for a schedule of events.

Large tulip poplars on Baldpate Mountain's steep slopes give the impression of old-growth forest, but the woods here are 80-year-old second-growth mixed hardwoods. Like most of New Jersey, until the 1930s and 40s the forest was cleared for agriculture and wood-based industry. Orchards, fallow fields and a farm pond remain. Remnants of Honey Hollow, a small nineteenth century settlement on the mountain's slopes, are still visible and now provide homes for chipmunks, mice and garter snakes.

American Redstart

Premier
★ SITE ★

Wildlife to Watch

Many forest-dwelling species breed here, including red-shouldered and red-tailed hawks, Cooper's hawks, yellow-billed cuckoo, northern flickers, Kentucky warblers, wood thrushes, veerys and eastern towhees. The preserve also provides critical migratory stopover habitat for warblers, vireos, thrushes, orioles and tanagers. Wintering species include brown creeper, Carolina and black-capped chickadee, pileated woodpecker and tufted titmouse. Wild turkeys are prevalent as are white-tailed deer. Look for groundhog and fox dens around the foundations of old buildings and along stone walls.

The old orchard and fallow fields around the visitor center are good places to see eastern bluebirds, Baltimore orioles, eastern kingbird, Carolina wrens, yellow-breasted chat and song sparrows. The woods are alive with warbler song from April through early June. Hike up one of the ridge trails to listen for hooded, black-throated green and black-throated blue warblers. Ovenbirds, great-crested flycatchers, gray catbirds, American redstarts, eastern towhees and scarlet tanagers are common. Gray squirrels scold from the treetops and white-tailed deer snort and stomp their feet at your intrusion. Listen for the call of wood frogs in early spring and northern gray treefrogs through June. The hawk migration is good here in the fall.

Audubon
IMPORTANT
BIRD AREAS

Trails

Washington Crossing State Park: There are 13 miles of moderately easy hiking trails located throughout the park. Easy trails at the nature center vary in length from 0.25 mile to 1 mile. Trails are not universally accessible. A 5-mile multi-use trail at the Phillips Farm Day Use Area is open for biking and 2.5 miles are partially open for horseback riding.

Over ten miles of trails for hiking, mountain biking and horseback riding traverse the north and south sides of Baldpate Mountain, running from the base of the mountain to the ridgetop. Go to www.njtrails.org for a trail map.

Site Notes   A fee is charged at Washington Crossing State Park. Call or check online for current information. Ted Stiles Preserve is free and trails are open sunrise to sunset, seven days a week.

Size   Washington Crossing: 3,126 acres

Ted Stiles Preserve: 1,100 acres

Directions   Washington Crossing State Park: From exit 1 on I-95, take NJ 29 north for 2.8 miles. Turn right onto Washington Crossing-Pennington Road and travel 0.7 mile to park entrance.

Premier
★ SITE ★

Ted Stiles Preserve: From exit 1 on I-95 take NJ 29 north for 4.8 miles to Fiddlers Creek Road. Turn right and travel 0.1 mile to entrance to the visitor center or 0.2 mile to a parking area at the trailhead on left.

Nearest Town Titusville

Ownership Washington Crossing State Park: NJDEP Division of Parks and Forestry

Ted Stiles Preserve: County of Mercer

Contact Washington Crossing State Park: 609-737-0623; www.njparksandforests.org

Ted Stiles Preserve-County of Mercer: 609-448-4947; www.nj.gov/counties/mercer/commissions/park/baldpate.html

Features scenic vistas, hiking, horseback riding, mountain biking, visitor center, restrooms, drinking water, parking, interpretive center, trails, interpretive programs, picnicking, cross-country skiing, camping

Red-spotted Purple Butterfly   PHOTO BY JOHN PARKE

PIEDMONT ■ *Washington Crossing State Park/Ted Stiles Preserve at Baldpate Mountain*

Premier
★ SITE ★

Striped Skunk

PHOTO BY BOB CUNNINGHAM

Rose-breasted Grosbeak

PHOTO BY JIM MALLMAN

Premier
★ SITE ★

Assunpink Lake

PHOTO BY LAURIE PETTIGREW/NJDFW

Description

This 5,664-acre tract is a wonderful example of the Piedmont physiographic region with its gently rolling hills, fertile fields and oak-hickory woods. Assunpink boasts three man-made lakes that provide valuable fish and wildlife habitat and serve as popular rest stops for migrating waterfowl in the fall.

Assunpink offers some of the best bird watching in central New Jersey. Look for grassland species in the extensive fields in spring and summer. This site provides habitat for numerous scrub-shrub and mixed-upland forest-dependent wildlife. Several species of owls and hawks frequent the fields and woods of the area. Northern harriers are particularly common during the fall and winter months. Walk the unmarked trails that traverse the fields for easy viewing of wildlife.

Wildlife to Watch

Pull into any of the grassy parking areas near the office. In the spring and summer these fields are home to grassland bird species, including grasshopper and vesper sparrows. Fall migration brings Lincoln's, white-crowned, lark and chipping sparrows. Red foxes and northern harriers cruise the fields hunting for smaller mammals like deer mice and meadow voles. Assunpink and Stone Tavern lakes contain largemouth bass, chain pickerel and pumpkinseed and are used by Canada geese, ruddy duck, common merganser, lesser scaup, pied-billed grebe and ring-necked duck during migration. Dabblers like green-winged teal, mallard, American black duck, northern shoveler, gadwall and American wigeon also frequent the lake. These lakes also attract osprey, herons, egrets and

PIEDMONT ■ *Assunpink Wildlife Management Area*

Great
▲ SITE ▲

the occasional tern. In the wooded areas along the lake edge are butterflies such as falcate orangetip, dreamy duskywing and red-banded hairstreak.

Long-eared owls are known to winter here and great horned and eastern screech owls can be seen all year. Wild turkey and white-tailed deer feed in the fields in early morning. Walk the field edges along the woods to see and hear white-eyed vireo, willow flycatcher, blue-winged warbler, rose-breasted grosbeak, orchard oriole, indigo bunting and blue grosbeak. The woods resound in spring with the calls of great-crested flycatcher, veery, black-and-white warbler, American redstart, hooded warbler, ovenbird and eastern towhee.

Audubon
IMPORTANT
BIRD AREAS

Trails

Many unmarked trails and old roads wind through the woods and fields.

Site Notes	The Division of Fish and Wildlife's central region office is located at Assunpink. Maps and information are available at the office. Assunpink is open for hunting during prescribed seasons.
Size	6,299 acres
Directions	From I-195, take exit 11. Go north on Route 43 (Imlaystown Road) for 1.2 miles. Turn right onto Eldridge Road at second stop sign (no road signs) and proceed straight for 0.5 mile to the WMA office on the right.
Nearest Town	Hightstown
Ownership	NJDEP Division of Fish, Game and Wildlife
Contact	609-259-2132; www.njfishandwildlife.com
Features	parking, hiking, horseback riding, boat launch, canoeing/kayaking

Juniper Hairstreak

PHOTO BY TONY MCBRIDE

Great
▲ SITE ▲

PIEDMONT ■ Assunpink Wildlife Management Area

119

White-tailed doe

PHOTO BY BOB CUNNINGHAM

Description

The peaceful, rolling hills of Monmouth Battlefield are a patchwork of fields, orchards and mixed-hardwood forest. The park is a National Historic Landmark where one of the largest battles of the Revolutionary War was fought on June 28, 1778. The park preserves this rural eighteenth-century landscape amidst increasing development and provides a haven for humans and wildlife alike. Two working farms grow grain and maintain a pick-your-own orchard. Over 100 species of birds inhabit or pass through the park during migration.

Wildlife to Watch

The rural, open landscape makes the park a great place to see grassland birds. Thirty acres of native grassland have been restored, and wet meadows containing showy wildflowers harbor a mix of butterflies and other interesting insects in summer and fall. Look for bobolinks and savannah sparrows in grassy fields in April and May. Dickcissels and vesper sparrows are rare but have been seen here. Eastern meadowlarks and grasshopper sparrows are present in spring and summer. Look for horned larks in fallow farm fields and low, grassy areas. Other than gray squirrels, mammals will be harder to see, but evidence of them is easy to find. Look for tracks, scratchings and scat of striped skunk, Virginia opossum and coyote. White-tailed deer can often be seen in the fields at dusk and dawn. Red-tailed hawks nest here and many other hawks are common migrants in the fall.

Great
▲ SITE ▲

Trails

There are over 25 miles of trails crisscrossing the fields and streams and running through the woods. Visitors can learn about history through interpretive signage while strolling the trails. Trails vary in length from 0.6 to 2 miles, are of rolling terrain and have a grass or dirt surface. There is a 0.7-mile universally accessible trail located at the visitor center. Horseback riding is permitted north of the railroad tracks.

Site Notes New Jersey Audubon Society offers weekend bird walks in spring, summer and fall. Deer hunting takes place during a special season in winter.

Size 1,818 acres

Directions From exit 8 on the New Jersey Turnpike, take NJ 33 east for 11 miles. Stay on NJ 33-Business when highway splits to park entrance on left in 0.1 mile.

Nearest Town Freehold

Ownership NJDEP Division of Parks and Forestry

Contact 732-462-9616; www.njparksandforests.org

Features visitor center, interpretive center, picnicking, restrooms, drinking water, hiking, cross-country skiing, horseback riding, scenic vistas, parking

Honeybee gathering pollen

PHOTO BY JIM MALLMAN

PIEDMONT ■ *Monmouth Battlefield State Park*

Great
▲ SITE ▲

Wildflower Meadow

PHOTO BY JOHN PARKE

Description

The Plainsboro Preserve provides critical migratory, nesting and wintering habitat for wildlife in the midst of suburban sprawl. Features include 50-acre Lake McCormack, a mature beech forest, scrub-shrub, wet meadows and a riparian floodplain corridor. The scrub-shrub areas represent New Jersey's changing land use patterns, as this area was once farmed but is now reverting to woodlands. More than ten rare or endangered plants grow within the preserve and over 150 species of birds have been recorded, including breeding Cooper's hawks.

Wildlife to Watch

In spring and summer, look and listen for both yellow-billed and black-billed cuckoos; it's a treat to be able to compare the two in close proximity. Spring migration also brings palm, prairie, yellow-rumped and yellow warblers. Blue grosbeaks breed here, as do common yellowthroats, American goldfinches, song sparrows, field sparrows and indigo buntings. The meadows explode with a profusion of wildflowers that attract butterflies, dragonflies and other insects. Fall migration is a great time to look for sparrows and finches. Check McCormack Lake for tree, rough-winged and barn swallows from April through August and large rafts of American black ducks, common mergansers, mallards, ring-necked and ruddy ducks in February. Bald eagles, great blue herons and green herons might be seen fishing the lake in any season. Sit on the deck behind the environmental center for a lakeside view. Take a walk through the woods in late winter/early spring to see white-breasted nuthatches, red-bellied woodpeckers and northern flickers.

Trails

Over five miles of trails wander along the shoreline of McCormack Lake and through the woods and meadows of the preserve. Trails are not paved but the terrain is easy to negotiate and relatively flat. The trails loop through a variety of habitats, making birding easy. The longest trail (blue) is 2.5 miles. Trails are open seven days a week, sunrise to sunset. Trail map and descriptions are available at www.njtrails.org.

Site Notes	The Environmental Education Center boasts an indoor tree house and an "under the pond" room. Call the center or check the website for hours of operation and upcoming events.
Size	1,000 acres
Directions	Take US 1 to the Scudders Mill Road exit in Plainsboro Township; exit onto Scudders Mill Road east and follow to the traffic light at the intersection with CR 614 (Dey Road). Turn left onto Dey Road. Follow to the first light (Scotts Corner Road). Turn left onto Scotts Corner Road and travel 1 mile to the entrance on the left.
Nearest Town	Cranbury
Ownership	County of Middlesex, Township of Plainsboro, New Jersey Audubon Society
Contact	609-897-9400; www.njaudubon.org
Features	interpretive center, interpretive programs, restrooms, drinking water, gift shop, trails, hiking, parking

Yellow-billed Cuckoo

PHOTO BY JOHN PARKE

Great
▲ SITE ▲

Scarlet Tanager

Description

Heavily forested Sourland Mountain stands amid cultivated fields interspersed with housing developments. Once a quarry where basalt was mined for use as railroad ballast and road beds, the forest consists mostly of second-growth oak trees. Like many forests in New Jersey, this one is not mature and exhibits the characteristic uniform canopy and undeveloped understory of a young forest.

Wildlife to Watch

Spring migration is an excellent time to look in the upland and wetland forests for neotropical songbirds. Listen for scarlet tanagers, Baltimore orioles, hooded warblers and wood thrushes. Spring wildflowers are abundant too. Look for reptiles and amphibians in the summer. Vernal pools form in shallow depressions creating habitat for spotted salamanders, wood frogs and spring peepers. The forest edge along the power lines is an excellent place to view Appalachian azure butterflies in May, whose larvae use black cohosh plants in the forest as host plants.

Trails

One main trail leads from one end of the preserve to the other. Three shorter trails create loops of varying lengths. The main trail is wide and mostly flat but the loop trails can be wet and require rock hopping across small creeks. Information and a trail map are available online.

Great
▲ SITE ▲

Site Notes This is a natural area with no facilities. Download the park brochure from the website before visiting. The park is open for deer hunting during prescribed seasons.

Size 273 acres

Directions From NJ 31/US Highway 202 in Ringoes, go east on CR 602 (Wertsville Road) for 3.5 miles. Turn right (south) onto CR 607 (Rileyville Road) and travel 1.7 miles up the mountain to a driveway on the left. Turn left and go straight up the center driveway to the parking area. A smaller parking area is located on Ridge Road. Go back down Rileyville Road to Ridge Road and turn right. The parking area is on the right in 0.5 mile.

Nearest Town Ringoes

Ownership Hunterdon County Park System

Contact 908-782-1158;
www.co.hunterdon.nj.us/depts/parks/guides/Sourland.htm

Features trails, hiking, parking, biking, cross-country skiing

Black Rat Snake   PHOTO BY LAURIE PETTIGREW/NJDFW

PIEDMONT ■ *Sourland Mountain Preserve*

Great
▲ SITE ▲

Description

This picturesque Wildlife Management Area located in the foothills of the Sourland Mountains boasts fallow fields, old fields succeeding to scrub-shrub, deciduous forest, a small mill pond and Alexauken Creek, which flows into the Delaware River in nearby Lambertville. The mosaic of habitats and location along the Sourland Ridge make this an important area for migrant and nesting birds.

Wildlife to Watch

Scan the fields for American tree sparrows, as well as chipping, field, grasshopper, savannah and song sparrows. Breeding birds include both black-capped and Carolina chickadees, rose-breasted grosbeaks, summer tanagers and winter wrens. Come at dusk in February and March to catch the dance of the timberdoodle, otherwise known as the American woodcock. Listen for the crescendo of the ovenbird and the lilting *ee-o-lay* of the wood thrush in spring. White-tailed deer, gray squirrels and eastern cottontails are the most commonly seen mammals.

Trails

There are many unmarked and unmaintained trails that wind through the fields and woods.

Site Notes: This is a natural area with no facilities. Maps of the area are available at the West Amwell Municipal Building at 150 Rocktown-Lambertville Road or online at www.njfishandwildlife.com/wmaland.htm.

Size: 689 acres

Directions: From the intersection of SR 31 and US 202 in Ringoes, travel south on US 202 for 0.6 mile to Route 179 south. Take Route 179 south for 0.5 mile to parking area on the left. For additional parking, from US 202 take Route 179 south for 0.4 mile to Gulick Road and turn left and take Gulick Road to its end. Turn right onto Rocktown Hill Road and in 0.1 mile, make a right onto Rocktown-Lambertville Road. Go 0.8 mile to parking area on right.

Nearest Town: Ringoes

Ownership: NJDEP Division of Fish and Wildlife

Contact: 973-383-0918; www.njfishandwildlife.com

Features: parking

John A. Phillips Preserve   50

Description

The John A. Phillips Preserve encompasses nearly 1,700 acres of forest, stream and wetlands. The preserve is located in the Spotswood outlier, a unique "island" of pine barren habitat. Dominant plants include pitch and shortleaf pines, scrub oaks and several members of the heath family, including high and lowbush blueberry, dangleberry and black huckleberry. The Phillips Preserve is also home to rare orchids like the pink lady's slipper.

Wildlife to Watch

Over 50 species of nesting birds have been identified, including pine and black-and-white warbler, yellow-billed cuckoo, scarlet tanager, veery, wood thrush and indigo bunting. Red fox and white-tailed deer are frequently seen, while evidence is often all that is seen of such underground denizens as eastern mole and antlion. The preserve is also home to the locally rare southern ring-neck snake, eastern box turtle and Fowler's toad. Look for spring azure, mourning cloak and little wood satyr butterflies in spring.

Trails

Nature Trail: (yellow blazes) 0.5 mile, easy, self-guided interpretive trail with brochures available at the trailhead

Pleasant Valley Trail (white blazes): 2.5 miles, moderate

Blueberry Flats (orange blazes): 1 mile, moderate

Old Bridge Sands Trail (blue blazes): 1.2 miles, moderate

Park Trails: 1 mile, paved

Site Notes: The park is open daily from dawn to dusk. Limited hunting is allowed for deer during prescribed seasons. A full schedule of park events is available at www.co.middlesex.nj.us/parksrecreation/conservcorp.asp

Size: 1,700 acres

Directions: Take NJ Turnpike exit 9 for New Brunswick. Follow Route 18 south for approximately 8 miles. Turn right onto Maple Street (Wawa Convenience Store on the corner). Park entrance is at the end of Maple Street. Park along soccer/football fields. Trailhead is at the far corner of the football field.

Nearest Town: Old Bridge

Ownership: Middlesex County

Contact: 732-745-3900; www.co.middlesex.nj.us/parksrecreation/index.asp

Features: restrooms, parking, trails, hiking, nature checklist

Mercer County Park Northwest and Rosedale Park 51

Description

This lovely little park attracts some very interesting species of grassland birds and wintering raptors. Known locally as the Pole Farm, it was the site of AT&T's transoceanic antenna, used to broadcast radio signals to Europe from the 1920s to 1975. Today, it consists of large, grassy fields interspersed with woods, streams and small ponds.

Wildlife to Watch

Birding is best here in spring, early summer and winter but there is always wildlife to see. Eastern bluebird, indigo bunting, American goldfinch, bobolink, eastern meadowlark, yellow warbler, field sparrow and red-tailed hawk breed here. Winter birds include northern harrier, long-eared owl, short-eared owl, northern saw-whet owl and white-crowned and tree sparrows.

PIEDMONT ■ *Other Sites*

Other sites

Trails

There are several short loop trails that join to make longer walks. Trails are level and marked and partially accessible. Some sections can be muddy during wet weather.

Site Notes: The park is open seven days a week from dawn to dusk. Both the Sierra Club (www.newjersey.sierraclub.org/central/) and the Washington Crossing Audubon Society (www.washingtoncrossingaudubon.org) lead regular field trips.

Size: 910 acres

Directions: Take exit 7 from I-295. Go north on US 206 for 0.3 mile to CR 546. Turn left and travel 1.8 miles and bear right onto Federal City Road. Take Federal City Road for 1.1 miles to Blackwell Road and turn right. Parking area is on the left in 0.2 mile. The park spans both sides of Blackwell Road.

Nearest Town: Lawrenceville

Ownership: Mercer County Park Commission

Contact: 609-448-4947; http://nj.gov/counties/mercer/commissions/park/

Features: parking, trails

Stony Brook-Millstone Watershed Association Reserve 52

Description

The Stony Brook-Millstone Watershed Association's mission is to improve the quality of the natural environment in the 265-square-mile watershed drained by the two rivers. The association addresses issues such as stream corridor protection and watershed management and uses the nature reserve to showcase land stewardship practices. Part of the reserve is leased to the Honey Brook Organic Farm, a community-run farm that grows organic produce for its members. Buttinger Nature Center offers educational programs and nature exhibits. The beauty of the Katie Gorrie Memorial Butterfly House should not be missed.

Some of the oldest trees in central New Jersey are found here, as well as such interesting species as red fox, coyote, long-tailed weasel and northern flying squirrel. Birders will enjoy looking out for osprey, bobolink, Cooper's hawk, red-shouldered hawk, or any of six species of owl that frequent the reserve.

Wildlife to Watch

In an effort to be good land stewards, the Association has installed bluebird, purple martin and wood duck nest boxes and planted native grasses to encourage grassland wildlife. Look for eastern bluebird, grasshopper sparrow, bobolink, American kestrel, eastern cottontail and groundhog. Watch for reptiles, amphibians and invertebrates at the pond.

Trails

Fourteen miles of trails wind through the reserve. Surfaces are dirt or grass over relatively flat terrain. Trails are open dawn to dusk, seven days a week. Trail maps and information about length and difficulty is available online or at the visitor center.

Site Notes: Buttinger Nature Center is open Tuesday through Saturday. Call for hours of operation.

Size: 860 acres

Directions: From NJ 31, north of Pennington, turn right (east) onto Titus Mill Road. Continue on Titus Mill Road for 1.2 miles to the reserve entrance, marked by a sign that reads "Watershed Nature Center."

Nearest Town: Pennington

Ownership: Stony Brook-Millstone Watershed Association

Contact: 609-737-7592; www.thewatershed.org

Features: visitor center, parking, trails, hiking, interpretive programs, restrooms, drinking water, cross-country skiing, picnicking, checklist

Turkey Swamp County Park   53

Description

Turkey Swamp Park, located in the far northern corner of the pine barrens, is primarily pitch-pine/oak/sweet gum forest with an understory of lowbush blueberry, dwarf huckleberry and catbrier. The high water table and sandy soil forms sphagnum bogs in the dips and hollows, creating a swamp-like feel, but there is no true swamp.

Wildlife to Watch

Doppler radar migration studies conducted by the New Jersey Audubon Society list this area as critical migratory stopover habitat for songbirds. The woods explode with early morning sound during spring migration. Common species include great-crested flycatchers, yellow-throated vireos, scarlet tanagers, Baltimore orioles and eastern wood-pewee. Listen for the *pizza* call of the Acadian flycatcher or the whinny of the northern flicker. Whip-poor-wills call just before first light and wild turkeys gobble just after. White-tailed deer and gray squirrel are the most commonly seen mammals, but red and flying squirrels are present too. Go outside on a still, spring night and listen for migrating birds.

Trails

Nine miles of multi-use and fitness trails traverse the park through a pine barrens-like ecosystem.

Site Notes: Canoes, kayaks, paddleboats and rowboats are available to rent in summer. The park is open for deer hunting during prescribed bow seasons. The campground is open from Mar. 15–Nov. 15; 732-462-7286.

Size: 2,455 acres

Directions: Take I-195 to exit 22. Turn left onto Jackson Mills Road going north. Follow Jackson Mills Road to CR 53 (Georgia Road), turn left and follow CR 53 for 1.7 miles to main park entrance on left.

Nearest Town: Freehold

Ownership: County of Monmouth

Contact: 732-462-7286; www.monmouthcountyparks.com

Features: camping, canoeing/kayaking, restrooms, drinking water, hiking, horse-back riding, mountain biking, picnicking, parking

Other sites

Atlantic Coast

★ Premier Sites

▲ Great Sites

● Other Sites

63
59
9
55
Middletown · 36
62 61
· Red Bank
· Long Branch
35
· Asbury Park
195 · Spring Lake
70 · Point Pleasant
· Lavallette
Toms River · 58
9
56
· Waretown
Barnegat · 57 Barnegat Light
· Surf City
Tuckerton · · Beach Haven
60
· Port Republic
54
· Absecon
Pleasantville · 30 · Brigantine
322 · Atlantic City

Garden State Pkwy

Home to some of New Jersey's most endangered birds

Forming a ribbon-like border along New Jersey's eastern edge, the Coastal region consists of barrier islands, broad, shallow bogs, tidal salt marshes and upland edges. Of all the landscapes in New Jersey, this region is the most dynamic. Its contours change noticeably from year to year and even from one day to the next. From the bleak harshness of the beach to the tangled lushness of mixed-hardwood uplands, the coast is teeming with wildlife and unique plant communities.

New Jersey's coast supports hundreds of species of fish, turtles and marine mammals. Whales and dolphins are common sights offshore. Gulls, plovers and sanderlings search for tasty morsels where the water meets the sandy beach. Least terns, black skimmers and piping plovers, some of New Jersey's most endangered birds, are able to coexist with people thanks to the help of dedicated biologists, volunteers and cooperative shore communities.

On the dunes, just behind the beaches, the vegetation is characteristically low-growing and consists of dunegrass, sea rocket, beach pea, cocklebur and seaside goldenrod. Meadow voles, white-footed mice and eastern cottontails are common enough to be prey for red and gray foxes. Skunks, raccoons and opossums populate the thickets and forests between and behind the dunes.

Dominant tree species include American holly, black cherry, Spanish oak, white oak, blackjack oak and red cedar. Beach plum, bayberry, juneberry, blueberry, catbrier and Japanese honeysuckle make up the shrub layer.

Fowler's toads, one of only a few species of coastal amphibians, frequent the rainwater pools between the dunes, where they are fed upon by garter, king and hognose snakes. Other coastal reptiles include fence lizards and eastern box turtles in the upland and northern diamondback terrapins, mud turtles and snapping turtles in the marshes and dune ponds.

Horned Lark   *PHOTO BY STEVE BYLAND*

Blue Claw Crab

New Jersey's coastline forms the eastern boundary of the Atlantic Flyway, the pathway used by birds migrating along the eastern seaboard. During migration, large concentrations of migrating songbirds and raptors crowd the shrub thickets, dune woodlands and wooded upland edges of marshes. Tidal marshes, sand dunes, coastal forests and mixed-hardwood uplands are home to a variety of wildlife, including white-tailed deer, muskrats, otter, raccoons, red and gray foxes, reptiles and insects. The extensive salt marsh ecosystem supports an amazing variety of breeding herons, egrets, wading birds, terns, gulls and a growing osprey population.

Human impact on the coastal landscape is becoming more severe as development replaces the dunes and barrier islands. Due to ever-increasing human encroachment, most coastal landscapes are able to support wildlife populations in only small, fragmented reserves. Two notable exceptions are Island Beach State Park and Sandy Hook, part of the Gateway National Recreation Area. Island Beach, with its extensive vegetated dune system and dune forest, is a prime example of how the barrier islands in New Jersey looked before development.

Photo by Dwight Hiscano

Northern Pintail

PHOTO BY BOB CUNNINGHAM

Description

Edwin B. Forsythe NWR is one of the oldest national wildlife refuges in the country. Set aside as a waterfowl refuge to protect American black duck and Atlantic brant, the refuge protects much more today. To date, 323 species of birds have been seen on the refuge. Wading birds, shorebirds, waterfowl, passerines and raptors utilize the tidal wetland and shallow bay habitats, barrier beaches, coastal dunes, pitch-pine lowlands, Atlantic white cedar bogs and pine-oak uplands that make up the more than 46,000 acres of a refuge system that extends 50 miles along the Atlantic coast.

Originally two separate refuges, the Brigantine NWR (established in 1939) and the Barnegat NWR (established in 1967) were combined in 1984 and named for conservation great Congressman Edwin B. Forsythe. The wetlands of the refuge were designated as a Wetlands of International Importance in 1986 under the Ramsar Convention. Eighty-two percent of the refuge is wetlands, with the remaining 18 percent including forested uplands, areas of scrub-shrub, old fields and remote barrier islands. Sixteen hundred acres of marsh are diked to form fresh and brackish water impoundments. A freshwater environment amidst the salt is irresistible to many species of ducks, herons, egrets, shorebirds, gulls and terns. The dikes at the Brigantine Division not only create acres of impounded water but also a fabulous, 8-mile-long auto trail that provides some of the most incredible wildlife watching in the U.S. A view of the Atlantic City skyline looms to the south across salt meadows and Reeds Bay as you take a leisurely drive around the impoundments.

More than 6,000 acres of the refuge are designated as the Brigantine Wilderness Area. Little Beach and Holgate, the last two remaining completely undeveloped

ATLANTIC COAST Edwin B. Forsythe National Wildlife Refuge

Premier ★ SITE ★

barrier beaches in New Jersey, are off-limits to people from April 1 to August 31 to protect sensitive nesting habitat for beach-nesting wildlife. The Holgate unit located at the end of Long Beach Island offers seasonal opportunities to observe dynamic plant and animal communities in a wilderness setting.

Most but not all of the refuge's public-use facilities are located at refuge head-quarters in Oceanville, which is open daily from sunrise to sunset. The main attraction is the Wildlife Drive around the impoundments. Two towers and a universally accessible observation deck located along the drive provide elevated vantage points, complete with optics, from which to look out over the pools. There are many other access points throughout the refuge that provide different types of viewing opportunities. Pick up a refuge brochure or print one online prior to your visit.

Wildlife to Watch

Some of the best bird-watching opportunities occur during spring and fall migrations; however, if you brave the winter winds from late December you can see upwards of 180,000 waterfowl using the impoundments. Very large portions of the American black duck, Atlantic brant and snow goose populations winter in the refuge. Other species include mallards, buffleheads, brant, greater scaup, northern pintails, green-winged teal, gadwalls and hooded mergansers.

Thousands of wading birds and shorebirds use the impoundments, tidal creeks and mud flats for feeding and resting during spring and fall migrations. Shorebird use peaks in the spring, and the most common species include sanderling, semipalmated sandpiper, dunlin, semipalmated plover, short-billed dowitcher, greater and lesser yellowlegs, ruddy turnstone, red knot, whimbrel and spotted and pectoral sandpiper. Wading birds include great blue heron, great egret, yellow and black-crowned night heron, cattle egret, little blue heron, American and least bittern and glossy ibis. Gulls and terns forage on the refuge as well.

Spring brings an influx of warblers and songbirds and includes many coastal nesting species like saltmarsh sharp-tailed sparrow, seaside sparrow and marsh wren. Other nesters include ovenbird, scarlet tanager, yellow-billed cuckoo, yellow warbler, Kentucky warbler, prairie warbler, blue-winged warbler, black-and-white warbler and pine warbler. From mid-April through the end of May the uplands ring with bird song.

Take particular note of the peregrine falcons at the Brigantine Division, often seen sitting on the tower between the west and east pools. Osprey nest on the numerous platforms built for that purpose. Bald eagles can be seen year-round, and occasionally golden eagles winter here. Other raptors that can be seen during the year include broad-winged, red-shouldered, red-tailed and sharp-shinned hawks, great horned, barn, barred and short-eared owls, turkey vultures and northern harriers. The Barnegat Division has an accessible boardwalk and deck overlooking freshwater wetlands where you can watch feeding and resting wading birds and shorebirds.

Over 30 species of mammals live on the refuge, but most will be difficult to see. Both red and gray fox are here, as well as coyote. Long and short-tailed weasels have been found. Eastern cottontail, white-tailed deer and gray and red squirrel, muskrat, chipmunk and whistlepig (groundhog) are easily seen, but the small mammals that so many of the raptors depend upon for food are difficult to find. The most commonly seen, or more likely heard, amphibians are Pine Barrens and Cope's gray treefrogs. Wood turtles and diamondback terrapins are the most common reptiles, although several species of snakes are present.

Audubon
IMPORTANT
BIRD AREAS

Trails

Leeds Eco-Trail, a scenic 0.5-mile walk through salt marsh and native woods, offers visitors a chance to view life on the edge of this ecotone. Segments of the trail are boardwalk, and the first 700 feet is barrier-free.

Akers Woodland Trail is a 0.25-mile easy-walking loop through upland forest and provides many seasonal opportunities to see migrating warblers.

Jen's Trail is a 0.75-mile loop over a gradual ascent to 40 feet above sea level. This trail provides great views and an opportunity to see forest species.

Blue-winged Warbler

PHOTO BY BOB CUNNINGHAM

Premier
★ SITE ★

Songbird Trail is a 2.2-mile trail through the uplands that can be combined with other trails to make longer loop options.

Eno's Pond is a 1-mile self-guided nature trail that loops its way through pine barrens to observation decks and a wildlife blind. The trail is a partnership between Ocean County Parks and Recreation and Forsythe refuge. A 0.5-mile portion of the trail is accessible.

Site Notes	Wildlife Drive brochures and bird checklists are available at the self-service information booth in the parking area across from refuge headquarters or online. Avoid the summer biting-fly season.
Size	46,000 acres
Directions	From the south: take Garden State Parkway north to Atlantic City Service Area at mile marker 41. Follow the sign and take the service road to Jimmie Leeds Road (CR 633 east). Turn right onto Jimmie Leeds Road. At the next traffic light, turn left onto Great Creek Road. Continue 3 miles to US 9 and proceed 0.6 mile on Great Creek Road to refuge entrance.
	From the north: take the Garden State Parkway south to exit 48 which will lead you to US 9 south. Continue south past Smithville. At the traffic light in Oceanville (Great Creek Road), turn left and continue 0.6 mile into the refuge.
Nearest Town	Oceanville
Ownership	U.S. Fish and Wildlife Service
Contact	609-652-1665; www.fws.gov/northeast/forsythe/
Features	checklist, parking, trails, visitor center, interpretive programs, interpretive signage, observation platforms, restrooms, drinking water

ATLANTIC COAST ▫ *Edwin B. Forsythe National Wildlife Refuge*

Premier
★ SITE ★

Short-eared Owl

PHOTO BY STEVE BYLAND

Least Bittern

PHOTO BY STEVE BYLAND

Premier
★ SITE ★

Photo by Bob Cunningham

Experience bird migration at Sandy Hook

Cedar Waxwing

PHOTO BY STEVE BYLAND

Description

Gateway National Recreation Area is situated on either side of New York Harbor, welcoming visitors with open arms. Sandy Hook, the New Jersey arm of the recreation area, stretches 5.5 miles into New York Bay and is richly diverse in its habitats and history. This, coupled with its juxtaposition as the northernmost point along the New Jersey coast, ensures the Hook's attractiveness to migratory wildlife and to people. Nearly 340 species of birds and more than 50 species of butterflies have been recorded here.

Sandy Hook displays all the barrier island ecosystems, from sandy beaches and coastal dunes to maritime forest, salt marsh and the estuary. Located on the Atlantic Flyway, the site teems with birds in spring and fall. Sandy Hook is a designated Natural Heritage Priority Site due to its importance as one of New Jersey's most significant natural areas.

The Hook and its sister unit in New York, Jamaica Bay, have a long and distinguished history. America's first lighthouse, Sandy Hook Light, has guided sailors around the hook since June 11, 1764. Forts Hancock, Wadsworth and Tilden, located in strategic positions at the mouth of the harbor, protected New York during World Wars I and II. The Coast Guard has manned a station here since the 1800s. Come explore Sandy Hook's abundant natural and historical resources.

Wildlife to Watch

This site represents one of the top ten spots for year-round wildlife viewing in New Jersey. A variety of waterfowl spends the winters here, and bayside sandbars are a favored haul-out site for harbor seals. Spring migration begins

ATLANTIC COAST ■ *Gateway National Recreation Area*

in March and reaches its peak in mid-April. Birds of all kinds are moving through, and it's often hard to know where to look first. Raptor flights are dominated by Cooper's and sharp-shinned hawk, merlin and American kestrel. Waterfowl can still be found in the sheltered coves along the bayshore, and pelagic species are moving north along the Atlantic. Look for American black duck, American brant, long-tailed duck, bufflehead, red-breasted mergansers, northern gannet and red-throated and common loons. In late April, beach plum comes into bloom, attracting Henry's elfin and juniper hairstreak butterflies. Other Hook specialties include falcate orangetip and the threatened checkered white butterfly.

May brings shorebirds, warblers and songbirds. As many as 20 different species of warblers can be seen here on a good flight day. Northern parula, yellow, magnolia, black-throated blue and green, palm, Blackburnian and American redstart are good bets. Also seen are cedar waxwing, blue-gray gnatcatcher, ruby-crowned kinglet, brown creeper, white and red-breasted nuthatch, red-eyed vireo and alder flycatcher. Peregrine falcons nest in the area and forage in and around Sandy Hook. Other breeding birds include osprey, eastern phoebe, white-eyed vireo, great-crested flycatcher, common yellowthroat, boat-tailed grackle, black-capped chickadee and brown thrasher. Beach nesters include endangered least tern, black skimmer and piping plover. Sandy Hook contains the largest nesting population of endangered piping plover in the state. American oystercatcher, herring and laughing gull, common tern, willet and clapper rail breed on the marsh.

July brings the arrival of southbound sandpipers like ruddy turnstone, sanderling, least and semipalmated sandpiper and black-bellied plover. Migrant songbirds that spend the winter in South America often pass through in August and September. October heralds the arrival of large numbers of raptors, thrushes, sparrows and blackbirds. Braving the cold winds in winter can net interesting species like red-necked grebe, Barrow's goldeneye, snow bunting, snowy owl and winter finches. Rafts of waterfowl numbering in the tens of thousands are often seen in the coves and bays. Beautiful red fox are the most visible mammal. Do not be tempted to feed them.

Trails

A paved, multi-use path extends for 5 miles along the length of Sandy Hook. Many other trails, both paved and unpaved, wander into various areas of the recreation area. The terrain is flat but surfaces may be sand or grass. Maps are available at the various visitor centers.

Site Notes   Sandy Hook is open daily from sunrise to sunset. Sandy Hook is extremely popular on summer weekends, so plan on arriving early or late in the day to avoid temporary closures due to traffic congestion. The former Spermaceti Cove Life-Saving Service Station contains exhibits and a bookstore. The center is open daily. Maps are available online.

The New Jersey Audubon Society's Sandy Hook Bird Observatory is open Tuesday-Saturday from 10 a.m. to 5 p.m. and Sunday 10 a.m. to 3 p.m. Call 732-872-2500 or go online (www.njaudubon.org/Centers/SHBO/) for info. A free, detailed birding map of Sandy Hook is available. Check the sightings log for up-to-date information.

Size 2,044 acres

Directions From the Garden State Parkway, exits 117 from the north or 105 from the south, follow New Jersey 36 east for approximately 12 miles directly into the recreation area. The visitor center is 2 miles from the entrance.

Nearest Town Highlands

Ownership U.S. National Park Service

Contact 732-872-5970; www.nps.gov/gate/planyourvisit/sandy-hook-hours.htm

Features visitor center, interpretive programs, interpretive signage, parking, restrooms, drinking water, trails, scenic overlook, hiking, biking, canoeing/kayaking, boat launch, checklist, food

Black Skimmer

PHOTO BY BOB CUNNINGHAM

ATLANTIC COAST ▪ *Gateway National Recreation Area*

Premier ★ SITE ★

Photo by Dwight Hiscano

Purple Sandpiper

PHOTO BY BOB CUNNINGHAM

Description

Island Beach is one of the few undeveloped barrier beaches on the Atlantic Coast, preserving 3,000 acres of an ecosystem that has nearly disappeared due to erosion and development. This narrow strip of land preserves unique barrier island shoreline and near-shore habitats including open beach, primary and secondary sand dunes, coastal dune forest, dense maritime forest, fresh-water wetlands, tidal marsh and the quiet waters of the Barnegat Bay Estuary. Island Beach is designated as a Natural Heritage Priority Macrosite because of the significance of its habitats. Island Beach Viewing Area encompasses Island Beach State Park, Sedge Island Marine Conservation Zone and Sedge Island Wildlife Management Area.

The island has a long and varied history which dates back to its use by Native Americans. Its major attractions are its beaches and its wildlife. At one time, two life-saving stations were in operation on the island; one now serves as an interpretive center. The area has long been a favorite spot for hunting, fishing, swimming, botanic study and wildlife watching. The island was once owned by steel magnate Henry Phipps who planned to develop it as an upscale resort, and the Phipps summer cottage now serves as the Governor's retreat. One of the old hunting camps on Sedge Island, part of Sedge Island Wildlife Management Area, was restored and is used by the NJDEP's Division of Fish and Wildlife as an environmental education center. The Sedge House, which can only be reached by boat, sits amidst the 1,600-acre Sedge Island Marine Conservation Zone.

ATLANTIC COAST ■ Island Beach Viewing Area

Premier ★ SITE ★

The Sedge Island Marine Conservation Zone, the first marine conservation zone in New Jersey, was designated to provide protection and management for the zone's natural resources. These resources are sensitive to disturbance, overuse and pollution. The marine conservation zone plays an important role in reducing user conflicts and protecting sensitive habitats. It encompasses the 192-acre Sedge Island WMA, a series of low marsh islands located behind the shelter of the barrier island. These islands teem with wildlife. The best way to experience this unique area is to take a canoe or kayak tour offered by the park's interpretive staff.

Wildlife to Watch

Island Beach presents great wildlife-viewing opportunities in all seasons. Spring migration brings a variety of warblers, shorebirds, songbirds and wading birds to the scrub-shrub thickets, maritime forest and salt marsh. The island has one of the largest osprey colonies in the state, and many of the nests are visible from the road. There are also beach-nesting least terns, black skimmers and piping plovers. Watch for diamondback terrapins crossing the road in May and June when they come ashore to lay their eggs. Look for evidence of raccoon, red fox and striped skunk in the telltale eggshells found around pilfered nests. Bottlenose dolphins are often visible from the beach.

Fall and winter are the best times to see rare birds and pelagic species. While you will see plenty with binoculars, this is the site for a scope. Stop at the first bath house and walk to the top of the boardwalk to scan the ocean for northern gannet, red-throated loons, scoters, gulls and possibly a black-legged kittiwake or parasitic jaeger. Fall and winter also bring sparrows, peregrines, merlins, horned larks, snow buntings and the occasional snowy owl. Keep watch as you drive south toward the end of the island. Park in the last lot and walk along the beach toward the inlet. Harbor and gray seals are frequently visible from the jetty areas, as are purple sandpipers and ruddy turnstones. Dunlin and sanderlings play tag with the waves as they feed along the surf line. Red foxes are ubiquitous and often seen on the beach. Please don't feed them, even when they beg!

A paddle through the conservation zone and around the Sedge Islands in spring and summer reveals species more typical of the salt marsh. Oystercatcher, great egret, peregrine falcon, diamondback terrapin, black-bellied plover, greater and lesser yellowlegs, American black duck, river otter and laughing gulls are representative of the species you might see.

Audubon
IMPORTANT
BIRD AREAS

Trails

Access is limited to existing trails to help maintain sensitive habitats. Please stay on the trails. The Island Beach State Park Discovery Trails System offers a self-guided experience through the nine plant communities of a barrier island. Wayside exhibits located along each trail interpret the natural and cultural stories of the park. There are eight trails, each less than 1 mile. Brochures and maps are available at the Park Office.

Horseback riding is permitted at Island Beach State Park from October 1 through April 30. There are 6 miles of ocean beach in the southern and central portions of the park available for equestrian use, and a parking area is designated for horse trailers during this time period. Reservations are required. Contact the park office at 732-793-0506.

Site Notes	An entrance fee is charged year-round.
Size	3,003 acres
Directions	From exit 82 on the Garden State Parkway, take NJ 37 east for 6.8 miles, crossing the causeway onto the island. Follow the signs for Seaside Park/Island Beach State Park around to the right. In 0.7 mile, you will be on Central Avenue. Continue on Central Avenue for 2 miles to the park entrance straight ahead.
Nearest Town	Seaside Park
Ownership	NJDEP Division of Parks and Forestry
Contact	732-793-0506, www.njparksandforests.org
Features	hiking, biking, horseback riding, restrooms, drinking water, food, canoeing/kayaking, observation blind, interpretive signage, interpretive center, visitor center, bath house, Coastal Heritage Trail Site

Harbor Seal

PHOTO BY BOB CUNNINGHAM

Premier ★ SITE ★

Harlequin Duck

PHOTO BY STEVE BYLAND

Description

Barnegat Lighthouse State Park is situated across the inlet from Island Beach State Park on Long Beach Island. The 172-foot-tall lighthouse, dubbed "Old Barney," has long guided sailors traveling up and down the coast. This 32-acre state park is one of the best places to see winter waterfowl, seabirds and mammals. Visitors who climb to the top of Barnegat Lighthouse are rewarded with a panoramic view of Island Beach, Barnegat Bay and Long Beach Island.

Visitors can learn about the changing nature of the coastline and the natural environment that surrounds the lighthouse, including Barnegat Bay, the Atlantic Ocean and the maritime forest. The forest, which is dominated by black cherry, sassafras, eastern red cedar and American holly, is an important resting and feeding area for migratory birds on their long journey to and from their breeding sites.

Wildlife to Watch

Barnegat Inlet is an extremely important area for wintering waterfowl. This is the only site in New Jersey to reliably see wintering harlequin ducks. Common eider, red-breasted merganser, long-tailed duck, common and red-throated loon and white-winged, black and surf scoters are common winter residents as well. The dunes and open sandy areas are utilized by American pipit, horned lark and lapland longspur in migration and during the winter. During the breeding season, a portion of the beach at the state park is fenced off to protect beach-nesting birds, including federally listed piping plovers and least terns. During spring and fall migration, songbirds utilize the small copse of maritime forest.

Trails

One of the last remnants of maritime forest on Long Beach Island is found at Barnegat Lighthouse State Park. The Maritime Forest Trail is a 0.2-mile-long, self-guided loop-trail through this unique environment.

Site Notes The lighthouse is open daily (weather permitting) from April 1 through October 31. The remainder of the year the lighthouse is only open on weekends. There is a per person fee to enter the lighthouse from Memorial Day through Labor Day. Visitors can also catch the views from the top without climbing the 217 steps thanks to four cameras that transmit live images of the view to a display in the adjacent interpretive center.

Size 32 acres

Directions From the Garden State Parkway exit 3, take NJ 72 east to Long Beach Island. Turn left and take Long Beach Boulevard north along Long Beach Island. Long Beach Boulevard becomes Central Avenue in the town of Barnegat Light. Continue north to Broadway. Turn left and follow Broadway to the end of the island and into the park.

Nearest Town Long Beach

Ownership NJDEP Division of Parks and Forestry

Contact 609-494-2016; www.njparksandforests.org

Features interpretive center, restrooms, parking, trail, scenic views, picnicking

Red-throated Loon

PHOTO BY BOB CUNNINGHAM

Great
▲ SITE ▲

Cattus Island County Park

PHOTO BY LAURIE PETTIGREW/NJDFW

Description

Cattus Island is actually a peninsula between Silver Bay and Barnegat Bay. The park contains more than 200 acres of tidal salt marsh, 100 acres of freshwater wetlands and 100 acres of upland forest. It is an ecological gem in the midst of much development. Extensive salt marshes with salt hay, cord-grass and pine-oak forests are interspersed with Atlantic white cedar swamps, maple-gum swamps and successsional fields. Don't miss the butterfly garden planted with an assortment of plants that bufferfly species like monarch, mourning cloak wild indigo duskywing and noctuid moths can't resist. Close to 300 plant species grow in the park, which also supports an amazing assortment of wildlife.

Wildlife to Watch

Start at Cooper Environmental Center by picking up a park map and tree identification guide. The center has an observation deck with a boardwalk which overlooks a salt marsh. Over 250 species of birds live on Cattus Island. Ospreys nest in the summer, waterfowl overwinter in the bays and wetlands, and songbirds, raptors and wading birds spend the year here. Look for bufflehead, canvasback, brant and all three mergansers on the bay in winter, sharp-shinned hawk, brown thrasher, white-eyed vireo, Carolina wren and yellow, blue-winged, black-and-white and pine warblers on walks through the pines, and clapper rails, great blue heron, snowy egret and willet in the salt marsh. River otter are often spotted early in the morning along with white-tailed deer. Signs of nocturnal creatures such as raccoons, striped skunk and Virginia opossum are visible if you look closely. Little brown bats and reptiles hibernate through winter but are commonly seen in the summer.

Trails

There are 6 miles of trails that traverse boardwalks, unpaved roads and dirt trails over mostly level terrain. The Hidden Beach Loop Trail (orange) is one of the most interesting trails, winding through the salt marsh and over a hummock on the edge of Barnegat Bay where a mansion once stood. The trails vary in length from 0.3 to 2.2 miles but can be combined for longer hikes. A short, universally accessible trail leaves from the parking area near the environmental center. Trail maps are available at the park or online.

Site Notes The park is open daily from dawn to dusk. Cooper Environmental Center is open daily. Call the center or check online for a listing of upcoming programs and events.

Size 497 acres

Directions From exit 82 on the Garden State Parkway, take NJ 37 east for 4.5 miles to Fischer Boulevard (CR spur 549). Take Fischer Boulevard. for 2.1 miles to Cattus Island Boulevard. Turn right and follow signs into the park entrance on the left.

Nearest Town Toms River

Ownership Ocean County Parks and Recreation

Contact 732-270-6960; www.ocean.nj.us/parks/cattus.html

Features trails, hiking, interpretive center, restrooms, drinking water, parking, interpretive signs, interpretive programs, observation platform, scenic overlook, picnicking, checklist

Brown Thrasher

Great
▲ SITE ▲

Cheesequake State Park

This ecotone between the outer and inner coastal plains teems with wildlife

Cheesequake State Park

PHOTO BY LAURIE PETTIGREW/NJDFW

Description

Cheesequake State Park is unique because of its geographical location. Situated between the urban north and the suburban south, it lies in an ecotone, a transitional zone between two different ecosystems. Open fields, salt and freshwater marshes, an Atlantic white cedar swamp, a small pine barrens and a stand of northeastern hardwood forest are found here. The 386-acre natural area is a striking example of vegetation change along a gradient from coastal salt marsh habitat to upland forest. Take one of the various trails running through the area to appreciate this ecotone. The natural area displays a diversity of plant species and community types characteristic of both northern and southern New Jersey.

The interpretive center is located just an easy walk from the parking area for the Red/Green/Blue trails. Learn about the three main habitats of the park and their wildlife through live animal displays, exhibits and public programs. As you enter the building, murals depict the three habitats and the plants and animals that are found in each. There are also exhibits about the Lenape Indians and the early colonists. The covered front deck is a perfect location for wildlife viewing.

Wildlife to Watch

Spring and fall migration is the best time to visit Cheesequake for wildlife viewing. Its proximity to the coast and varied habitats ensure its popularity as a migratory stopover site. More than 186 species of birds have been sighted at the park, so pick up a bird checklist at the center and head out to the trails. The woods, fields, cedar and hardwood swamps ring with bird sounds on spring mornings. Warblers, vireos and thrushes abound. Scan the marsh for

Great
▲ SITE ▲

great blue heron, red-winged blackbird, nesting osprey, northern harrier, willet, muskrat and northern diamondback terrapin. Blue crabs are found during late summer in Hook's Creek. Woodland mammals include gray squirrel, eastern chipmunk, raccoon, striped skunk, red and gray fox and occasional white-tailed deer. Waterfowl utilize the wetlands all year but particularly October through March.

Trails

There are five designated trails at the park. The Red, Yellow, Green and Blue trails are for hiking only, while the White Trail is designated for hiking and mountain biking. Trail lengths range from 1.5 to 3.5 miles, and trail difficulty ranges from easy to moderate with inclines. The longest trail takes about 90 minutes to walk over various terrains. Trail guides are available at the interpretive center or park office. Pink lady's-slipper orchids grow along the Yellow Trail in spring.

Site Notes The interpretive center provides free weekly interpretive programming focusing on a variety of seasonal topics. Consult the Parks and Forestry Calendar of Events online or call the center for details at 732-566-3208. The center is open Wednesday through Sunday, 8 a.m. to 4 p.m., and seven days a week from Memorial Day through Labor Day when staffing permits.

Size 1,569 acres

Directions From exit 120 on the Garden State Parkway, turn right on Matawan Road. Travel 0.5 mile to Morristown Road. Turn right and go 0.7 mile to Gordon Avenue. Turn right and go 1 mile into the park.

Nearest Town Matawan

Ownership NJDEP Division of Parks and Forestry

Contact 732-566-2161; www.njparksandforests.org

Features interpretive center, trails, camping, hiking, biking, fee, boat launch, canoeing/kayaking, interpretive programs, picnicking

Canada Geese

PHOTO BY STEVE BYLAND

Great
▲ SITE ▲

Great Bay Boulevard WMA

PHOTO BY LAURIE PETTIGREW/NJDFW

Description

Created in 1932 to link Tuckerton and Atlantic City, Great Bay Boulevard was intended to cross Great Bay. The project, which was never finished, spans miles and travels through a vast expanse of salt marsh to Great Bay. The state now manages it as a Wildlife Management Area. An old Coast Guard Station at the end of the road serves as a research lab for Rutgers University. The view from each of the five bridges along the road is breathtaking.

Tuckerton Seaport is a working maritime village bringing New Jersey's maritime traditions to life through living history exhibits and activities. The seaport is home to the Barnegat Bay Decoy and Baymen's Museum. A hiking, biking and driving tour along Great Bay Boulevard begins at the seaport.

Walk or drive across the street to Tip Seaman Park to scan Lake Pohatcong for waterfowl, herons and egrets. The renowned Ocean County Decoy Show here each September features wildlife artists and decoy carvers.

Wildlife to Watch

Salt marshes are among the most productive ecosystems on earth, and this 5,000-acre tract is teeming with wildlife, with over 160 species of birds documented on the peninsula. Snails rise and fall along the blades of cordgrass with each tide and are eaten by American black duck and clapper rail. Glossy ibis, whimbrels and willets feast on fiddler crabs along the banks at low tide. Little blue herons, snowy egrets and tri-colored herons fish the creeks in all tides. Diamondback terrapins appear to be flotsam as they float in the creeks

Great
▲ SITE ▲

with just their heads poking out of the water. Look for yellow-crowned and black-crowned night heron roosting in trees and shrubs during the day. Warblers and songbirds move through the shrub thickets and maritime forest during spring and fall migration. Listen for the burbling call of the marsh wren and the hot-metal hiss of the Nelson's sharp-tailed sparrow in summer. Check the creeks in winter for bufflehead, scaup, ruddy duck and hooded, red-breasted and common merganser. Look for northern harrier hunting over the marsh during the day and short-eared owl at dusk. The cedar hummocks are home to white-tailed deer, red fox, river otter and raccoon.

Trails

Start at Tuckerton Seaport to take an easy walk along the 0.5-mile maritime forest trail. From there, you can hike, bike or drive along Great Bay Boulevard to Great Bay. The road is seven miles long and makes a great bike ride. Guide books with a bird list can be purchased in the gift shop. Kayak trails are also depicted in the guide book, and there are several good launch sites along the boulevard. Guided tours and rentals are available at some local marinas.

Site Notes	If you visit in summer, prepare to become intimately acquainted with the biting greenhead fly.
Size	Great Bay Boulevard WMA: 5,507 acres
	Tip Seaman Park: 40 acres
	Tuckerton Seaport: 22 acres
Directions	Take Garden State Parkway exit 58 and go east on CR 539 for 5 miles. Turn right onto US 9 south. The entrance to Tip Seaman Park is 0.25 mile on the right; the entrance to Tuckerton Seaport is on the left.
Nearest Town	Tuckerton
Ownership	Great Bay WMA: NJDEP Division of Fish and Wildlife
	Tip Seaman Park: Ocean Co. Dept. of Parks and Recreation
	Tuckerton Seaport: Tuckerton Seaport Organization
Contact	Great Bay Boulevard WMA: 609-259-2132; www.njfishandwildlife.com
	Tip Seaman Park: 609-296-5606; www.ocean.nj.us/parks/tipseaman.html
	Tuckerton Seaport: 609-296-8868; www.tuckertonseaport.org
Features	restrooms, drinking water, hiking, biking, interpretive center, visitor center, interpretive programs, scenic views, canoeing/kayaking

Great
▲ SITE ▲

Hartshorne Woods

61

Description

This hilly, prominent site sits at one of the highest points along the Atlantic Coast. From high on Rocky Point, there is an incredible view overlooking the Navesink and Shrewsbury tidal rivers, across Sandy Hook and all the way to the Atlantic Ocean. This forest contains a unique combination of oak, American sycamore and tulip poplar, along with a remnant of the once-plentiful maritime holly forest.

Wildlife to Watch

Birding is splendid here in the spring when migrating warblers, flycatchers and thrushes stop to feed on the insects nectaring on tree flowers. Osprey, belted kingfisher, bank swallow and egrets feed in and over the water in the summer, and waterfowl winter in the rivers.

Trails

Hartshorne Woods has the most extensive and challenging series of trails in the Monmouth County Park System. Over 19 miles of trails are open for hiking, biking and horseback riding. The view from Rocky Point is worth the mile-long walk, although the terrain is challenging. The trails are moderate to steep and mostly paved. Trail maps are available at the kiosk in the parking area or online.

Site Notes: The park is open dawn to dusk seven days a week.

Size: 787 acres

Directions: From exit 105 on the Garden State Parkway, take NJ 36 east to NJ 35 north. Go north on NJ 35 for approximately 5 miles to Navesink River Road (CR 12A). Turn right and continue 4.7 miles. Turn right onto Locust Road. Cross Clay Pit Creek Bridge to a five-way intersection. Bear right onto Navesink Avenue and continue to the park.

Nearest Town: Highlands

Ownership: Monmouth County Park System

Contact: 732-842-4000; www.monmouthcountyparks.com

Features: trails, restrooms, hiking, biking, horseback riding, cross-country skiing, camping, scenic overlook

Huber Woods

62

Description

This beautiful little park is nestled on a hill overlooking the Navesink River. In 1974, the farm and home at Huber Woods were donated to Monmouth County and transformed into a park. The farmhouse and outbuildings now serve as an environmental center and a reptile house. Set in a mixed-suburban/rural landscape, the farm's oak-maple-hickory woods and pastureland can be explored on 6 miles of trails. The environmental center, just uphill from the park system's Equestrian Center, serves as an information stop on the New Jersey Coastal Heritage Trail.

Wildlife to Watch

Start at the environmental center and check out the feeders which often attract pine siskin and winter finches. The deciduous woods attract the normal woodland species like downy, hairy and red-bellied woodpecker, blue jay, Carolina chickadee, white-breasted nuthatch, great-crested flycatcher, eastern towhee and eastern wood-pewee. In the fall, look for migrating birds and butterflies. Native plants highlight the Discovery Path, a 0.25-mile-long, barrier-free trail south of the environmental center. A guide is available at the center. Frogs and toads breed in the pond in spring, and wildflowers blossom with butterflies in the summer.

Trails

There are 7 miles of trails winding through the various habitats of the park. Trails are rated from easy to challenging and vary in length. Trail maps are available at the center.

Site Notes: The environmental center and the Reptile House are open seven days a week. Call for hours of operation.

Size: 366 acres

Directions: From NJ 35 in Middletown, travel east on Navesink River Road, just north of the Cooper Avenue Bridge, for 2.8 miles to Brown's Dock Road and turn left (north). Park entrance is at the top of the hill.

Nearest Town: Navesink

Ownership: Monmouth County Park System

Contact: 732-872-2670

Features: interpretive center, interpretive programs, trails, hiking, horseback riding, restrooms, parking, picnicking, scenic overlook

Old Bridge Waterfront Park   63

Description

This lovely little park inhabits over a mile of Raritan Bay shoreline and boasts a 1.3-mile walking/biking path along the waterfront. Raritan Bay is an important waterbird feeding and wintering area, and there are often huge mixed flocks of birds on the bay. Walk out on one of the fishing piers for marvelous views of Raritan Bay, or stroll through the natural area or along the beach.

Wildlife to Watch

The best time to see waterbirds is October through March. Those who brave the wind and cold are often rewarded with good looks at a variety of species of grebes, loons, geese, gulls, ducks and occasionally harbor seals. Count on seeing species like horned and pied-billed grebe, canvasback, and redhead ducks, common, black and surf scoters, greater black-backed gull, ruddy duck, red-breasted merganser, double-crested cormorant and common and red-throated loon. Bonaparte's gull and black-legged kittiwake are frequent visitors. Bring a spotting scope to view rafts of ducks on the bay.

Size: 52 acres

ATLANTIC COAST *Other Sites*

Other sites

Directions: From the Garden State Parkway going north, take exit 120. Turn left on Matawan Road/Laurence Parkway (CR 626) and travel to intersection with NJ 35. Cross NJ 35 and travel straight to the parking area on the bay.

From Garden State Parkway going south, take exit 129 for US 9 south. US 9 and NJ 35 merge at base of the Edison Bridge and then divide. Stay on NJ 35 south for approximately 3 miles. Cross over a drawbridge and make a quick right at its base. Follow the jughand under NJ 35 and stay on the service road to park entrance on the left.

Nearest Town: Laurence Harbor

Ownership: Middlesex County

Contact: 732-745-3900; www.co.middlesex.nj.us/parksrecreation/old.asp

Features: restrooms, parking, trails, walking, biking, scenic views

Ring-necked Duck

Expanding ranges of wildlife
An opportunity to practice environmental stewardship

The coastal waters of New Jersey are frequently inhabited by marine mammals, including harbor seals (Phoca vitulina) and bottlenose dolphins (Tursiops truncatus). Harbor seals can be seen year-round in New Jersey, whereas coastal bottlenose dolphins migrate seasonally along the mid-Atlantic coast.

In the summer of 2008, several bottlenose dolphins took up residence in the Shrewsbury/Navesink River system in northern New Jersey after following prey fish into the area. The dolphins, the focus of great interest and attention, were carefully documented and assessed by federal and state wildlife officials. Although the dolphins were in good health and observed eating and behaving normally, some community members, concerned the river system was not an appropriate habitat for the animals, pressured wildlife officials to intervene. However, the experts agreed the presence of the dolphins was a cause for celebration, not concern, as bottlenose dolphins historically inhabited New Jersey coastal waters and may have left when the habitat could no longer support them.

Careful management of the fish prey stocks and the dolphin population over the past several years appears to have enabled both populations to rebound, and the dolphins may be a good sign that the ecosystem has improved. As wildlife species expand their range in response to conservation efforts and changing ecosystems, local communities will have increasing opportunities to view and appreciate nature and to practice good environmental stewardship.

For more information: www.nmfs.noaa.gov/pr/health/njdolphins/

Bottlenose dolphin in the Shrewsbury/Navesink River system in summer 2008

PHOTO BY NOAA SOUTHEAST FISHERIES SCIENCE CENTER

Other sites

Pine Barrens

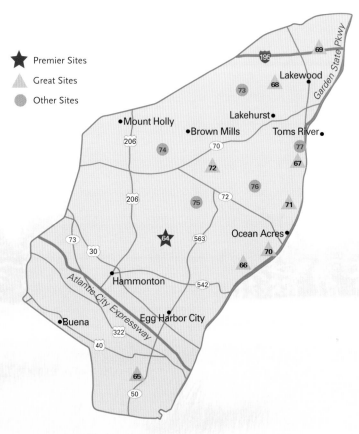

Premier Sites

Great Sites

Other Sites

195

69

Lakewood

73

68

●Mount Holly

Lakehurst●

206

●Brown Mills

Toms River●

74

70

77

72

67

76

206

72

75

72

71

73

564

563

Ocean Acres●

30

70

66

Hammonton

542

●Buena

322

Egg Harbor City

40

65

50

The Pine Barrens support plants found in few other places on earth

The New Jersey Pine Barrens, also known as the Pinelands, is a 1.4-million-acre, mostly forested area of the state's outer coastal plain. Early European settlers deemed the area "barren" because the sandy, acidic, nutrient-poor soil would not support the crops they had brought with them. The Pine Barrens, however, is far from barren; its unique soils and hydrology support distinctive and diverse plant communities and a variety of rare plants, including orchids and carnivorous plants.

Seldom rising more than 100 feet above sea level, the New Jersey Pine Barrens lies in a broad, flat surface within the state's outer coastal plain, bordered on the east by the Atlantic coast and on the west by a cuesta or low ridge. The Kirkwood-Cohansey Aquifer, containing 17 trillion gallons of water, lies beneath the surface sands. Over its geologic history it has experienced

American Robin   PHOTO BY JIM MALLMAN

warm periods and ice ages, and this portion of New Jersey was alternately submerged beneath the rising ocean or exposed when water was frozen into the polar ice caps. It is believed that because of this constant disruption, the current plants and animals of the pine barrens ecosystem arrived here within the last 12,000 years or since the last retreat of the glaciers that blanketed northern New Jersey.

Human influence has had a significant effect on the New Jersey Pine Barrens. Early settlers harvested timber for boats, houses and other wood products. Later, as the bog iron and glass furnace industries grew, so did the demand for charcoal to fuel them—resulting in the clear-cutting of vast acres of forest. Other early Pine Barrens products included sand, gravel, paper, turpentine and sphagnum moss. The original Atlantic white cedar swamps were cleared of the giant trees for shipbuilding and shingles; today modern cranberry bogs occupy the former wetland swamps. It was in the New Jersey Pine Barrens that the blueberry was first successfully domesticated and cultivated. As the industries of the Pine Barrens folded and the majority of people left the region, the forests gradually returned. Blueberries and cranberries are still significant exports, with New Jersey being the third-largest producer of cranberries in the country.

Today the New Jersey Pine Barrens is recognized as a national and international treasure. Most of the region is protected and included within the overlapping 1.1 million-acre Pinelands National Reserve, created by the National Parks and Recreation Act of 1978, and the 927,000-acre Pinelands Area, designated by the state Pinelands Protection Act of 1979. The Act limits development in most of the Pinelands Area, provides safeguards for endangered and threatened species and adds a measure of protection against contamination and overuse of the aquifer.

The New Jersey Pine Barrens' many tea-colored streams and rivers provide ample opportunities to explore it by canoe or kayak—perhaps the best way to experience the flavor and unique ecosystems of this wild area. Visitors can also enjoy hiking and camping in addition to watching wildlife.

Pine Snake

PHOTO BY LAURIE PETTIGREW/NJDFW

Photo by Laurie Pettigrew/NJDFW

Eastern Box Turtle

Description

Wharton State Forest encompasses over 115,000 acres in the heart of the Pinelands National Reserve and is the largest tract of publicly-owned land in New Jersey. It is a major component of the largest remaining contiguous forest block in the state. The area is composed of mature pine forest, oak forest, pine-oak forest, Atlantic white cedar swamps, tupelo-maple swamps and fallow cranberry bogs. The Mullica, Oswego, Wading and Batso Rivers flow through Wharton on their way to the Atlantic.

In 1978 the Pinelands National Reserve was created to protect the unique natural and cultural resources of the New Jersey Pine Barrens. Unbroken forests of pine, oak and cedar make this the largest tract of open space on the mid-Atlantic coast. The New Jersey pine barrens' uniqueness springs from its water. The sandy soil allows water to pass through quickly and be stored in the aquifer below. Slow moving streams, fed by the 17-trillion-gallon Cohansey Aquifer, supply the marshes and bays of southern New Jersey with water.

As habitat for most animals, the Pine Barrens is indeed barren. The area's physical and biotic characteristics create a harsh environment with low habitat diversity, limiting the variety of animals found here. Fish and amphibians are especially limited because of the extreme acidity of the Pine Barren's cedar water. However, there are certain amphibians that are well adapted to the area because of the tolerance they've developed to acidity. In fact, the Pine Barrens is the only place in New Jersey where carpenter frogs and Pine Barrens treefrogs are found.

Batso Village, on the eastern fringe of the state forest, was a bog iron and glassmaking industrial center from 1766 to 1867. This historic village reflects the agricultural and commercial enterprises that existed there during the late

PINE BARRENS ▪ Wharton State Forest

Premier
★ SITE ★

165

nineteenth century. The restored village consists of 33 historic buildings and an interpretive center that offers exhibits and programs about the historic and natural resources of the New Jersey Pine Barrens.

All that remains of old Atsion Village is the Greek Revival mansion built in 1826, standing like a roadside sentinel at the site of the once-thriving village. The Atsion Recreation Center, on the opposite side of Route 206, consists of a public beach, rental cabins, a nature trail and picnic area and is open April 1 through October 31.

Wildlife to Watch

Only a select variety of plants and animals are able to tolerate the acidic streams of Wharton State Forest. Look in the vegetation at the margins of lakes and in the backwaters of streams for the brightly colored black-banded sunfish. Another interesting Pine Barrens fish is the eastern mudminnow, which hides in dense vegetation. The mudminnow is a facultative air-breather, which means that although it has gills for breathing under water, it can also survive during periods of low water by using its gas bladder to breathe air. The aquatic larvae of northern red salamanders are plentiful in Pine Barrens streams; look for adults that remain near the streams' margins to guard the developing young. Be aware of gnawed trees along the rivers as evidence of beaver activity. River otters and long-tailed weasels are rarely seen but are present along the streams. Raccoons and gray foxes are also common throughout the area.

Reptiles are plentiful throughout the New Jersey Pine Barrens. The most common turtles are the terrestrial eastern box turtle and the aquatic painted, spotted and snapping turtles. Stinkpot and redbellied turtles are also frequently seen. The most common snakes are northern water snakes, scarlet snakes, black racers, eastern hognose snakes, common kingsnakes, milk snakes and rough green snakes. The area's sandy soil attracts burrowing snakes such as pine, scarlet, hognose and worm snakes. Water-filled hollows under the roots of cedars are used as winter dens by eastern timber rattlesnakes.

Listen for the cheery *drink-your-tea* of the eastern towhee as it searches noisily for food amongst fallen leaves. Other common birds of the upland areas include blue jay, Carolina chickadee, pine warbler, scarlet tanager, black-and-white warbler and eastern towhee. Listen at dusk for common nighthawks, whip-poor-wills and Chuck-will's-widow. Look in low areas of dense vegetation along streams or rivers for gray catbirds, yellow warblers, yellowthroats, American redstarts and field sparrows. Herons, egrets and ducks frequent the rivers and lakes. Red-winged blackbird, swamp sparrow and song sparrow live among the emergent vegetation surrounding lakes.

Trails

One of the best ways to experience the New Jersey Pine Barrens is by canoe. Miles of river run through Wharton State Forest and more than a dozen nearby outfitters offer canoe rentals. The 50-mile-long Batona Trail, marked with pink blazes, stretches from Ong's Hat in Brendan T. Byrne State Forest through Wharton State Forest to Bass River State Forest. The trail crosses several roads and can be reached by car at many points, making it possible to enjoy different types and lengths of hikes. There is a self-guided 1.5-mile nature walk around Batsto Lake. Over 500 miles of sand roads and unmarked trails offer unlimited possibilities for exploration. Trail maps are available at park headquarters.

Site Notes Batsto Village and Atsion Recreation Area are open daily (Atsion is closed in winter). An entrance fee is charged from Memorial Day to Labor Day. Wharton State Forest is open for hunting in prescribed areas. There is no fee to visit the state forest.

Size 115,111 acres

Directions From US 30 in Hammonton, take County Route 542 east for 8 miles. The entrance to Wharton Visitor Center and Batsto Village is on the left. To reach Atsion Village and Recreation Area: From the intersection of US 206 and US 30 in Hammonton, travel 7.5 miles north on US 206. The entrance is on the left.

Nearest Town Hammonton

Ownership NJDEP Division of Parks and Forestry

Contact 609-561-0024; www.njparksandforests.org

Features visitor center, interpretive programs, interpretive signs, camping, trails, hiking, biking, horseback riding, canoeing/kayaking

Common Nighthawk

Premier
★ SITE ★

Painted Lady Butterfly   *PHOTO BY STEVE BYLAND*

Description

Native Americans were the first inhabitants of this land but it was eventually owned by the Estell family, who built a glassworks in the 1800s. With the advent of World War I it became the site of a munitions plant. After 70 years the forest has reclaimed this area, and it is now home to an incredible diversity of plants and animals. Freshwater wetlands, ponds, creeks, upland fields, pine-oak forests and hardwood swamps are ready to be explored by those willing to hike.

Wildlife to Watch

Special wildlife enhancement areas like the butterfly garden and Cribber's field attract American goldfinch, eastern bluebirds and swallowtail, buckeye and angelwing butterflies. Typical Pine Barrens reptiles and amphibians, including Pine Barrens treefrog, northern pine snake and corn snake live here too.

Duck Farm Road takes you to Tin Box Road and the dam of an energetic beaver who may be working hard to cover the road with a pond. For a drier hike take Frog Pond Road to a wildlife enhancement area and Swamp Trail. The 1.5-mile-long loop trail from the nature center winds through a hardwood swamp and upland forest and past several ponds. Turtles, frogs, snakes and insects make their homes at the ponds from spring through early fall. Raccoons, white-tailed deer and red foxes, whose dens are just off the trail, visit the ponds. The observation deck overlooking Stephens Creek is on the boundary between a freshwater marsh and the oak-pine forest. Ospreys and

Great
▲ SITE ▲

belted kingfishers are often seen fishing along the creek, and river otters use the bank as a slide. The swamps are alive in spring with neotropical songbirds.

Trails

There are nearly 20 miles of hiking trails through all types of habitats over flat and sandy but firm, terrain. Trail descriptions and a map are available at the nature center or online.

Site Notes The park and nature center are open daily. The park is partially open for hunting during certain prescribed seasons. Bikes and helmets can be rented at the nature center.

Size 1,700 acres

Directions From exit 17 of the Atlantic City Expressway, take NJ 50 south for approximately 6 miles to the entrance of Estell Manor park on the left. The nature center and parking area are on the right after a short distance.

Nearest Town Mays Landing

Ownership Atlantic County, Division of Parks and Recreation

Contact 609-645-5960; www.aclink.org/PARKS/mainpages/estell.asp

Features interpretive center, interpretive programs, trails, hiking, biking, cross-country skiing, restrooms, drinking water, picnicking, canoeing/kayaking, boat launch

Corn Snake   PHOTO BY JOHN PARKE

Great
▲ SITE ▲

Red Squirrel
PHOTO BY JIM MALLMAN

Description

Bass River State Forest was New Jersey's first state forest, acquired in 1905. Lake Absegami (67 acres) was created by the Civilian Conservation Corps (CCC) in the 1930s to provide additional recreation. Absegami Natural Area displays a pine-oak wood and Atlantic white cedar bog typical of the outer coastal plain. Bass River also contains the West Pine Plains Natural Area, part of a unique stunted forest ecosystem known locally as the pygmy pines. The mature forest grows only four to ten feet tall. The pine plains are globally rare and New Jersey boasts the largest acreage of this ecosystem in the world.

Wildlife to Watch

The Pine Barrens support fewer species of wildlife because of the harsh conditions, but many interesting species can be found here. Pied-billed grebe, hooded merganser and ring-necked duck can usually be seen on Lake Absegami in winter. Look for wood ducks, green heron, spotted, solitary and possibly pectoral sandpipers in spring and summer. Painted or spotted turtles, leopard frogs and carpenter frogs sun along the bank of the lake. Walk along the trail through the cedar bog in spring and listen for prothonotary and black-throated green warblers, Acadian flycatchers and northern waterthrush. Northern saw-whet owls breed here. Many of the common mammals are small and hard to detect, like the red-backed vole, the meadow jumping mouse and the southern bog lemming. Beaver, eastern cottontail and red squirrel are more frequently seen, or at least their signs are. The Argos skipper (a butterfly) occurs in the park but may be difficult to find.

PINE BARRENS ■ *Bass River State Forest*

Great
▲ SITE ▲

Trails

Eight easy walking trails range from 1 to 3.2 miles in length; none are universally accessible. The 0.5-mile self-guided Absegami Trail winds through Absegami Natural Area. All trails start at the second parking lot at the beach. A trail brochure is available at the office or on the portion of the Pink Trail near East Greenbush Road.

The 50-mile Batona trail runs from here through Wharton and Brendan T. Byrne State Forests. This easy walking trail is well marked with pink blazes. It passes through once-bustling but now forgotten towns with names like Four Mile, Butler, Martha and Washington.

Site Notes A public boat launch is located north of the recreational area parking lot. Only electric motors or manually-powered boats are allowed. A rowboat concession is operated during the summer months. Hunting is allowed in some parts of the state forest during prescribed seasons. There is an entrance fee.

Size 27,635 acres

Directions From southbound Garden State Parkway take exit 52, bear right at fork and make right onto East Greenbush Road (following brown forest trailblazer signs). Go to next intersection and make right onto Stage Road. Follow Stage Road approximately 1 mile to entrance on left.

From northbound Garden State Parkway take exit 50 (which puts you on Route 9 north), go straight through traffic light in New Gretna, follow Route 9 north and make left onto East Greenbush Road. Take East Greenbush Road over the Garden State Parkway to "T" intersection and make a right onto Stage Road; go approximately 1 mile to entrance on left.

Nearest Town Tuckerton

Ownership NJDEP Division of Parks and Forestry

Contact 609-296-1114; www.njparksandforests.org

Features trails, restrooms, drinking water, picnicking, hiking, camping, horseback riding, biking, canoeing/kayaking, entrance fee, visitor center, interpretive programs

Fence Lizard *PHOTO BY LAURIE PETTIGREW/NJDFW*

Great
▲ SITE ▲

Eastern Towhee

PHOTO BY STEVE BYLAND

Description

Double Trouble State Park offers an outstanding example of the Pine Barrens ecosystem and a window into New Jersey's Pine Barrens history. The park protects and interprets nearly 8,000 acres of significant natural, cultural and recreational resources representative of the Pinelands National Reserve. The park incorporates the 200-acre historic district of Double Trouble, once a company town centered around the harvest of Atlantic white cedar and the cranberry industry. The village contains 14 original buildings, and some of the cranberry bogs are still harvested each fall by a local farmer. Pristine Cedar Creek runs the length of the park, providing water for the cranberry bogs. Habitats include working and fallow cranberry bogs in various stages of succession, cultivated blueberry fields, bottomland hardwood swamp, Atlantic white cedar swamp and pine-oak uplands. Many plants unique to the Pine Barrens can be seen here.

Wildlife to Watch

Take the trail past the bog to Mill Pond Reservoir to see wood ducks in summer and ring-necked ducks and lesser scaup in winter. Look for tree swallows and purple martins casting for insects in summer and belted kingfishers all year. Snapping turtles often float just below the water surface with their heads peeking up. Northern water snakes might be seen sunning themselves on logs or along the banks. Along the way you may see or hear house wren, cedar waxwing, gray catbird, brown thrasher, pine warbler, chipping sparrow or eastern towhee. There are nesting veery, Acadian flycatcher and hooded warbler in the hardwood swamp. Listen for the *see-see-see-suzy* of the black-throated green warbler or the "squeaky wheel" call of the black-and-white warbler in the cedar bog. With luck you could see gray fox pups learning to hunt in June and July. Little brown bats begin feeding on insects at dusk in spring through fall.

Trails

The Double Trouble State Park Nature Trail is a 1.5-mile self-guided loop trail on which both natural and historical items are delineated and interpreted in the trail guide. The trail passes cranberry bogs and Atlantic white cedar swamps. Trail guides are available at the trailhead in the historic village. A dirt road leads from the parking area to the reservoir in 0.4 mile. In addition there are more than 28 miles of unmarked sand roads, closed to vehicular traffic, that serve as multi-use trails for hiking, biking and horseback riding.

Site Notes	Stay on trails and sand roads to avoid ticks and chiggers. Biting insects can be annoying during warmer months. Hunting is allowed in some areas of the park during prescribed seasons. None of the roads or parking areas is paved.
Size	7,881 acres
Directions	From southbound on the Garden State Parkway, take exit 77. Turn left at end of ramp onto Double Trouble Road south and travel straight into park entrance. From GSP northbound, take exit 77. Turn left at end of ramp and travel 0.25 mile to park entrance on left.
Nearest Town	Berkeley Township
Ownership	NJDEP Division of Parks and Forestry
Contact	732-341-4098, 732-341-662; www.njparksandforests.org
Features	hiking, biking, horseback riding, trails, parking, restrooms, visitor center, canoeing/kayaking

White-throated Sparrow

Great
▲ SITE ▲

Forest Resource Education Center

PHOTO BY JIM MALLMAN

Description

The New Jersey Forest Service operates the Forest Resource Education Center (FREC). The headwaters of historic Toms River flow through hardwood swamps and pine-oak uplands heading to Barnegat Bay. There are many habitats represented within this 660-acre site, including old fields, pine savannahs, deciduous woodlands and riverine bottomlands. The center offers conservation education programs promoting tree benefits and forest stewardship. The New Jersey Forest Tree Nursery occupies 45 acres of the site, where some 300,000 seedlings are grown annually for reforestation projects. A demonstration rain garden attracts birds and insects.

Wildlife to Watch

Start at the rain garden to look for ruby-throated hummingbirds and a variety of butterflies. Move on to explore the swamp for wood ducks, American redstart, eastern phoebe, black-throated green warbler and Louisiana waterthrush. Look for signs of beaver activity and the scat of river otter (it has lots of fish scales). In spring the swamp resounds with the mating calls of wood frogs and spring peepers. Ribbon snakes are common but not often seen because of their size and great camouflage. Raccoons often hunt along the banks of Toms River; look for their tracks in the mud. As you move through the upland areas of the site, look and listen for pine warblers, chipping sparrows, eastern wood-pee-wees and Carolina chickadees. Red-tailed hawks breed here and red-shouldered hawks and American kestrel are occasional visitors. Listen for screech and great horned owls at dusk and dawn in winter and whip-poor-will in spring.

Trails

There are seven miles of trails located in the northeast quadrant of the Forest Resource Education Center. Four of these trails are universally accessible and several of the trails have interpretive signs and interactive kiosks. You must use your five senses to navigate the sensory trail. All trails are easy to walk and offer good and varied viewing opportunities. Check out the bluebird trail for good looks at eastern bluebirds. Bluebirds may remain all year but the best time to see them is April through July. Horseback riding is permitted on the yellow trail.

Site Notes The dirt road into the center may be rough. Stay on trails to avoid ticks, chiggers and poison ivy. Parts of the Forest Resource Education Center are open to hunting during prescribed seasons.

Size 660 acres

Directions From I-195 take exit 21. Travel south on CR 527 for 6.2 miles. Turn right onto Bowman Road and go 0.9 mile. Turn right on Don Connor Boulevard and go 0.3 mile. Turn right into the entrance and take the dirt road to the parking area.

Nearest Town Jackson

Ownership NJDEP Division of Parks and Forestry

Contact 732-928-0936; www.njforestrycenter.org

Features trails, hiking, interpretive center, interpretive programs and signage, scenic overlook, horseback riding, biking, picnicking

Carolina Chickadee

PHOTO BY JIM MALLMAN

Great
▲ SITE ▲

Summer Tanager

PHOTO BY BOB CUNNINGHAM

Description

The 770-acre Manasquan Reservoir provides water for surrounding communities. The site contains 1,200 acres of woods and wetlands, where wildlife of all kinds is plentiful. In addition to providing water, the reservoir site provides a natural setting for recreation and outdoor pursuits. There is a thriving warm-water fishery and ample opportunities to explore by boat. An environmental center features nature exhibits and a nature trail.

The forests are an interesting mix of pin, oak, maple and sweetgum species. Six man-made wetlands and wildflower meadows support hundreds of species of migrating landbirds during spring and fall migration and abundant waterfowl in the winter and spring. Standing timber was left along the edges of the reservoir and provides habitat for black crappies. Pea-sized gravel was spread along the northern shore to provide spawning areas for largemouth and smallmouth bass and sunfish. Stump fields were left on the bottom, and cabled trees were anchored to provide structure for a variety of fish.

Wildlife to Watch

More than 20 varieties of fish, 20 types of mammals, 25 different species of reptiles and amphibians and 200 species of birds inhabit the reservoir and its surroundings. Take the perimeter trail for good views of resident and migratory waterfowl, particularly in the fall, and nesting and wintering bald eagles. Osprey nest on the reservoir. Scan the standing timber for wood ducks spring through fall. Other waterfowl include Canada geese, gadwall, American black

PINE BARRENS ■ Manasquan Reservoir

Great
▲ SITE ▲

duck, mallard, northern shoveler, ring-necked duck, hooded and common merganser and ruddy duck. The second-floor observation deck on the visitor center is a cozy spot for watching winter wildlife.

Park naturalists offer 40-minute weekend boat tours from Memorial Day through Labor Day. Visitors can expect to see double-crested cormorant, great blue and green herons, belted kingfisher and painted turtles up close.

Audubon
IMPORTANT
BIRD AREAS

Trails

There is a 5-mile, multi-use perimeter trail around the entire reservoir and the 1-mile Cove Trail at the environmental center. The perimeter trail is unmarked but easy to follow over a flat, gravel surface with a few slight inclines.

Site Notes All boats must launch from the visitor center and the purchase of a daily or seasonal launch pass is required. Boat tours and boat rentals are also available at the visitor center. The environmental center is open daily. Free nature programs are offered on most weekends. Call 732-751-9453 for information about these programs.

Size 1,203 acres (plus the 720-acre reservoir)

Directions From Interstate I-95, take exit 28 to NJ 9 north. Travel on NJ 9 north for 0.1 mile to light at Georgia Tavern Road. Turn right and proceed 0.3 mile to Windeler Road. Turn right and proceed 1.5 miles to the reservoir entrance on your left. For the environmental center, stay on Georgia Tavern Road for less than 1 mile.

Nearest Town Farmingdale

Ownership Monmouth County Park System

Contact visitor center: 732-919-0996

environmental center:
732-751-9453;
www.monmouthcountyparks.com

Features visitor center, interpretive center, interpretive programs, boat launch, canoeing/kayaking, hiking, trails, biking, vending machines, restrooms, drinking water

Canada Goose *PHOTO BY JIM MALLMAN*

Vegetation of a fire-adapted ecosystem   PHOTO BY LAURIE PETTIGREW/NJDFW

Description

Pine-oak forest predominates in the Stafford Forge Wildlife Management Area, featuring pitch pine, blackjack oak and southern white cedar as the primary trees. The unique plant and animal communities present here are due to the historic frequency of fires.

Native Americans burned extensively to improve hunting conditions and until the early 1900s the forest was clear-cut by settlers for firewood, charcoal and lumber. Over time the cycle of burning and cutting eliminated many plants that had grown along the margins and favored the rare plants we see in the Pine Barrens today. A unique assortment of plants and animals, including the curly grass fern, broom crowberry, eastern timber rattlesnake and the Pine Barrens treefrog live in this managed area.

For species to thrive in a fire-prone area, individuals must either survive fires or produce young that become established after the fire. Blueberries, pitch pines and oaks have underground stems or roots that survive fires. The above-ground parts of the plant may be killed, but after the fire they regenerate. The pitch pine sprouts from roots and has serotinous cones, which only open to disperse their seeds after a fire. The trunks of pitch pines may be scorched during a fire, but the thick bark prevents the fire from killing the underlying cambium layer. For animals to survive a fire they typically must either burrow or flee.

The pygmy pine forest on the northern plains is a dense stand of dwarf but mature pitch pine, blackjaw oak and scrub oak trees. Most of the oak trees originated as sprouts after fires, and many have two or more trunks. The uppermost crowns have been snapped off by strong winds and the lower branches have developed a new oddly shaped crown. These trees are important as nest and feeding sites for many wildlife species.

Wildlife to Watch

Travel north from the entrance by foot or in the car along the sand road that passes along the east side of a chain of four ponds. Each pond is separated by a dam, which you can walk or drive across. At the northern end of the last pond near the marsh are trees that have been gnawed upon by beaver. Look for hog-nose snakes, southern leopard frogs and northern water snakes in the spring and summer. Wintering birds include wood thrushes and American black ducks. Take a walk in the spring woods and look and listen for blue-winged warbler, brown thrasher, eastern towhee, eastern wood-pewee, pine warbler, prairie warbler, whip-poor-will, Baltimore oriole, black-and-white warbler and black-billed cuckoo.

Trails

No marked trails but many sand roads are suitable for walking. Driving may require four-wheel drive.

Site Notes The Stafford Ford Wildlife Management Area is a natural area with no facilities. Be careful driving on sand roads. Stafford Forge is open for hunting during prescribed seasons.

Size 11,529 acres

Directions From Garden State parkway exit 58, take CR 539 north for 0.2 mile. Turn right at the 4-mile marker. Go 1.6 miles to WMA entrance straight ahead. For the viewing platform in the pygmy pine forest, stay on CR 539 north toward Warren Grove for 2 more miles. The platform and trail are on the right.

Nearest Town Stafford Forge

Ownership NJDEP Division of Fish, Game and Wildlife

Contact 609-259-2132; www.njfishandwildlife.com

Features parking, hiking, biking

Baltimore Oriole *PHOTO BY BOB CUNNINGHAM*

Great
▲ SITE ▲

Pine Barrens Treefrog

Description

At over 900 acres, Wells Mills is the largest park of Ocean County's extensive park system. Vast pine-oak forests are interspersed with Atlantic white cedar swamps and hardwood swamps of red maple and sour gum trees. Wells Mills Lake, like all lakes in the New Jersey Pine Barrens, is man-made. The three-story nature center has great displays of local wildlife, New Jersey Pine Barrens culture and the history of Wells Mills as well as an observation deck on the third floor that offers a splendid view of the lake and the surrounding area.

Wildlife to Watch

White-tailed deer, raccoons, red and gray foxes, Fowler's toads, northern fence lizards, eastern hognose snakes and eastern box turtles are all residents here. Ring-necked ducks frequent the lake during the fall and winter. Rent a canoe (in-season) or take the 0.7-mile walk from the nature center to the waterfowl observation blind to look for American black duck, mallard, wood duck and Canada geese. Keep an eye out for red-bellied and painted turtles sunning themselves on fallen logs in spring and summer. Eastern mud and snapping turtles are commonly sighted in shallow waters, as are pickerel frogs. Listen for the *quonk, quonk* of the Pine Barrens treefrog at dusk.

A springtime walk through the pine-oak forest should reveal species such as the gray catbird, Carolina chickadee, white-breasted nuthatch, yellow-billed cuckoo, mourning dove, red-bellied woodpecker, eastern towhee and great-crested fly-catcher. Enjoy the cool air of the Atlantic white cedar swamp on a warm spring day and listen for eastern phoebe, eastern wood-pewee and pine warbler.

PINE BARRENS ■ *Wells Mills County Park*

Great
▲ SITE ▲

Trails

The park has over 17 miles of hiking trails of varying lengths and difficulty. There is also a trail for visually impaired people that emphasizes the senses of smell, hearing and touch. Trail maps are available at the nature center or online.

Site Notes The park and nature center are open daily. Canoes can be rented at the nature center May through October.

Size over 900 acres

Directions From the Garden State Parkway, take exit 69. Turn left (west) onto CR 523 (Wells Mills Road) and travel approximately 2.5 miles to park entrance on the left.

Nearest Town Waretown

Ownership Ocean County Parks and Recreation

Contact 609-971-3085; www.oceancountyparks.org

Features biking, hiking, trails, canoeing/kayaking, restrooms, interpretive center, interpretive programs, universally accessible, picnicking, drinking water

Red-bellied Woodpecker

PHOTO BY STEVE BYLAND

Great
▲ SITE ▲

Cranberry bog

PHOTO COURTESY OF WWW.HOGANPHOTO.COM

Description

Whitesbog Village, a historic cranberry and blueberry farming village, depicts early life in the Pine Barrens. Cranberries and blueberries are the only two native American fruits grown in wetlands. The Lenape Indians were the first people to harvest cranberries in New Jersey, using the wild red berry as food, medicine and as a symbol of peace. Cranberries depend on a fragile combination of wetlands soils, geology and climate, but it is not unusual to find 75 to 100-year-old bogs still in cultivation.

The Whitesbog Preservation Trust and Burlington County College's Pinelands Institute for Natural and Environmental Studies provide interpretive programs for school groups and visitors.

Brendan T. Byrne State Forest is located in the heart of New Jersey's Pine Barrens. Originally named after the Lebanon Glass Works, a thriving 1800s business, the name now honors the governor who helped preserve the Pine Barrens. Abundant sand and locally produced charcoal made the manufacture of high quality window glass possible here. However, once the timber supply for charcoal-making was exhausted, the factory was abandoned and reclaimed by the forest.

Wildlife to Watch

Cranberry wetlands recharge and filter groundwater, control floods and retain storm water. Winter flooding of active bogs attracts one of New Jersey's few large populations of tundra swans. Abandoned bogs provide dense habitat for

PINE BARRENS ■ *Whitesbog Village/Brendan T. Byrne State Forest*

Great
▲ SITE ▲

bald eagle, great blue heron, osprey, wild turkey and rare plants, including Pine Barrens bellwort and pitcher plants.

Dense stands of Atlantic white cedar are found along the forest's streams. The pine-oak woods are a favorite nesting place for red-headed woodpecker and home to timber rattlesnake and pine, corn and scarlet snakes.

Pine warblers arrive in March, followed by common nesters like eastern bluebirds, eastern towhees, tree swallows and whip-poor-wills. You might see little and big brown bats, white-tailed deer, red and gray foxes and red squirrels. Nowhere else in New Jersey can you observe tundra swans at such a close range. View these magnificent swans from your car by following any of the old bog roads leading out of the village, as they prefer the abandoned, flooded cranberry bogs. In February over 500 swans can be seen.

Trails

More than 25 miles of marked trails, with various trails and loops, provide a variety of hiking opportunities. The Mount Misery Trail allows mountain biking. The Cranberry Trail is universally accessible, with two easy loop trails of 1 and 2 miles leaving the parking area at the forest office. The 50-mile long Batona Trail links Brendan T. Byrne, Wharton and Bass River State Forests. Other trails intersect with the Batona Trail to provide loops of about 6 miles and 14 miles for day hikes.

Site Notes	Be careful driving on sandy roads. No trespassing on active cranberry bogs.
Size	Brendan T. Byrne State Forest: 36,647 acres
	Whitesbog: 2,500 acres
Directions	Whitesbog Village: From the junction of NJ 70 and CR 530, take CR 530 west towards Browns Mills for 1.2 miles. Turn right at the entrance to Whitesbog Village and continue 0.5 mile to parking area.
	Brendan T. Byrne State Forest Office: Located one mile east of the 4 Mile Circle on NJ 70. Turn at the forest entrance sign on NJ 70 and continue 0.6 mile to parking area.
Nearest Town	New Lisbon
Ownership	NJDEP Division of Parks and Forestry.
Contact	NJDEP: 609-726-1191; www.njparksandforests.org
	Whitesbog Preservation Trust: 609-893-4646; www.whitesbog.org
Features	interpretive programs, trails, hiking, camping, picnicking, biking, canoeing/kayaking, cross-country skiing

Great
▲ SITE ▲

Colliers Mills Wildlife Management Area

Description

Colliers Mills is primarily a largely unfragmented pitch pine-scrub oak forest and scrub/shrub habitat typical of a Pine Barrens ecosystem. Several small lakes and Atlantic white cedar swamps add interest and diversity. The Division of Fish and Wildlife maintains a number of large, fallow fields that attract grassland species of wildlife. Colliers Mills is considered to be a significant migratory stopover site for songbirds.

Wildlife to Watch

Approximately 70 species of birds nest on Colliers Mills including Acadian flycatcher, Baltimore and orchard oriole, ovenbird, blue grosbeak, state threatened savannah and grasshopper sparrow and the state endangered vesper sparrow. Many species of waterfowl and wading birds frequent the lakes. Look also for painted and snapping turtles, carpenter frogs and northern water snakes. You might see a pine or hognose snake sunning in a sandy opening in the forest or come across a fence lizard basking on a log on a cool morning. Butterfly species include brown elfin, eastern tailed-blue, Juvenal's duskywing, dotted skipper and bog copper.

Audubon
IMPORTANT
BIRD AREAS

Trails

There are no marked trails but a series of sand roads run throughout the WMA making for good walking and wildlife watching and they provide access to the three main lakes.

Site Notes: This is a natural area with no facilities. Colliers Mills is open to hunting during prescribed seasons.

Size: 12,662 acres

Directions: From I-195 take exit 16 to CR 537 west Follow CR 537 west for approximately 5 miles to CR 539. Turn left onto CR 539 south and go approximately 3 miles to Colliers Mills Road (CR 640). Turn left and go 0.9 mile to WMA entrance straight ahead.

Nearest Town: New Egypt

Ownership: NJDEP Division of Fish and Wildlife

Contact: 609-984-0547, www.njfishandwildlife.com

Features: parking, hiking, canoeing/kayaking, biking

Dot and Brooks Evert Memorial Nature Trail

74

Description

The Dot and Brooks Evert Memorial Nature Trail provides a rare opportunity to walk into the heart of an old swamp forest. In addition, this site vividly depicts the transition from inner coastal plain to a Pine Barrens ecosystem. The mature hardwood forest showcases diverse populations of interior forest species, including several varieties of ferns and orchids. A mixed-hardwood oak forest characterizes the vegetation of the inner coastal plain, while Atlantic white cedar, red maple, sour gum and pitch pine are characteristic of the Pine Barrens.

Wildlife to Watch

This viewing site contains an ecotone, an area where two distinctly different ecological communities blend, in this case inner coastal plain and Pine Barrens. At Station 3, where two forest types blend together, look for prothonotary and hooded warblers. Look in the swamp forest for Kentucky warblers, white-eyed vireos, blue-winged and worm-eating warblers and ovenbirds. Rough green snakes are abundant here but difficult to detect. Look for signs of flying squirrels and long-tailed weasels. Hermit thrushes, scarlet tanagers and red-eyed vireos, in addition to gray foxes and opossums, eat the fruit of the black gums in the fall. American robins and cedar waxwings feed on holly berries during the winter months.

Trails

There is a 1.75-mile interpretive nature trail complete with a trail guide, which is available at the parking area kiosk.

Site Notes: Boardwalks protect fragile wetlands, but much of the trail can be muddy.

Size: 170 acres

Directions: From US 206 south of Mt. Holly, take CR 530 east for 2.7 miles to CR 644 (Magnolia Road). Bear right and go 4.5 miles to CR 642 (Ongs Hat-Buddtown Road). Turn right and go 1.4 miles to small parking area on right.

Nearest Town: Pemberton Borough

Ownership: New Jersey Conservation Foundation

Contact: 908-234-1225; www.njconservation.org

Features: parking, trails

Franklin-Parker Preserve   75

Description

The Franklin-Parker Preserve is a former cranberry farm located in the heart of the New Jersey Pine Barrens, surrounded by 250,000 acres of state-owned land. This rare ecological treasure is home to more than 50 rare, threatened and endangered plants and animals. With almost 5,000 acres of wetlands and 4,000 acres of pine-oak dominated forest, there is much to see. The area is crisscrossed by old sand roads open for walking and biking. This site offers some of the most spectacular vistas of a Pine Barrens ecosystem found anywhere in New Jersey.

Wildlife to Watch

All the typical Pine Barrens wildlife is present here, including northern pine snake, Pine Barrens treefrog and barred owl. Bald eagles can be seen any time of the year. Cooper's hawk, American kestrel, northern bobwhite, wood duck, northern harrier and red-headed woodpecker all breed here. Listen

Other sites

also for calls of black-billed cuckoo, Acadian flycatcher, great-crested flycatcher and blue-winged warbler. Bobcats are known to use the area but are very secretive. Look for beaver and river otter signs near wetlands.

Trails

There are many access points located along CR 563 and CR 532 and some 50 miles of sand roads throughout. See website for most recent information and maps.

Site Notes: The preserve was purchased in 2003 and currently is being developed. Workshops and educational programs are offered occasionally. Check www.njconservation.org for updated information and an event schedule.

Size: 9,400 acres

Directions: From the Garden State Parkway take exit 50 (northbound) or exit 52 (southbound) onto US 9. Follow US 9 into the center of New Gretna. Take CR 679 north (Maple Avenue) for 8.5 miles to CR 563 north. Turn right and follow CR 563N for 6.5 miles. Parking area is on the left just before the entrance gate.

Nearest Town: Chatsworth

Ownership: New Jersey Conservation Foundation

Contact: 908-234-1225; www.njconservation.org

Features: trails, hiking, biking, parking, interpretive programs

Greenwood Forest Wildlife Management Area 76

Description

All three major habitats typical of the Pine Barrens occur in Greenwood Forest: upland pine-oak forests, Atlantic white cedar bogs and acidic streams and ponds. Most of this area is pine-oak forest interspersed with a few hundred acres of fields and scrub oak.

Wildlife to Watch

Webb's Mill Bog is an ideal location for observing Pine Barrens reptiles, amphibians and the unique plants found only in this harsh environment. Listen and look for Pine Barrens treefrogs in late spring and early summer, especially on warm, rainy nights. Endangered northern pine snakes and eastern timber rattlesnakes are residents of the wildlife management area. Songbirds typical of these pine-oak forests include pine warblers, Carolina chickadees, tufted titmice and white-breasted nuthatches. Look for great blue herons in the wetlands during summer, and listen especially for eastern towhees, which are present throughout the area. Butterflies include bog copper, Georgia satyr, hoary elfin, two-spotted skipper and oak hairstreak.

Audubon
IMPORTANT
BIRD AREAS

Trails

A boardwalk and trail with interpretive signs wind through Webb's Mill Bog, but there are no other marked trails. However, there are miles of sand roads to explore. A topographical map is helpful when exploring.

Site Notes: The Greenwood Forest Wildlife Management Area is a natural area with no facilities. Be careful driving on sandy roads. Greenwood Forest is open for hunting during prescribed seasons.

Size: 29,762 acres

Directions: From exit 58 on the Garden State Parkway take CR 539 north. Go approximately 15 miles to a parking area and sand roads leading to the fields.

Webb's Mill Bog: continue on CR 539 for approximately 4 miles to a pull-off on the right at a sign for Greenwood Forest WMA. The trail begins immediately on the right.

Nearest Town: Whiting

Ownership: NJDEP Division of Fish, Game and Wildlife

Contact: 609-259-2132; www.njfishandwildlife.com

Features: trails, hiking, biking, interpretive signs

Jakes Branch Park 77

Description

This 450-acre park serves as Ocean County's "Gateway to the Pine Barrens." The many exhibits in the magnificent nature center feature the nature and history of the New Jersey Pine Barrens. Also featured are five-story tall observation towers, live animal displays, and a bird and butterfly garden.

Wildlife to Watch

The tower provides the perfect vantage point for viewing raptors and vultures soaring on thermals. Eastern bluebirds nest in boxes supplied by local scouts. Look also for warblers, finches, sparrows, swallows and wrens. Listen for spring peepers, Pine Barrens treefrogs and Fowler's toads in spring. Eastern worm snakes are common.

Trails

A well-marked, 4-mile hiking trail begins near the parking area and travels through various Pine Barrens habitats over flat terrain on natural surfaces.

Site Notes: Open dawn to dusk. The nature center, which serves as a welcome center for the New Jersey Pine Barrens, is open daily except on major holidays.

Size: 450 acres

Directions: From the Garden State Parkway south take exit 77. Turn right at the end of the ramp onto Double Trouble Road. The park is 1.5 miles on the left.

From Garden State Parkway north, take exit 77. Turn left at the end of the ramp onto Pinewald-Keswick Road (CR 618). Go 0.5 mile and turn right onto Double Trouble Road. The park is 2 miles on the left.

Nearest Town: Toms River

Ownership: Ocean County Parks and Recreation

Contact: 732-281-2750; www.oceancountyparks.org

Features: visitor center, trail, hiking, picnicking, interpretive programs, interpretive signs, interpretive center, restrooms, drinking water, observation platform, observation tower, checklist

PINE BARRENS ■ *Other Sites*

Other sites

Lower Delaware River

Premier Sites

Great Sites

Other Sites

A freshwater tidal river
meets the brackish estuary

The Lower Delaware River region lies within the inner coastal plain, separated from the outer coastal plain by a belt of low hills running southwest across the state from Sandy Hook to Lower Alloway. These hills are remnants of a landform called a cuesta (a ridge of sedimentary rock), which rises to a height of nearly 400 feet in some areas. From this high point, the inner coastal plain slopes gradually south and west toward the Delaware River and Estuary. The Delaware, named in 1610 by Captain Samuel Argall for Virginia Governor Lord De La War, forms the western border of this region. Two ecologically distinct sections of the estuary are in the Lower Delaware Region—the fresh-water tidal river from Trenton Falls to Camden and the brackish upper estuary from Camden to the Cohansey River. The estuary has numerous fresh and brackish water marshes and provides habitat for many species of birds, fishes, reptiles, amphibians and mammals.

The soils of this region are made up of unconsolidated sands, silts, clays and gravels. This soil is generally more fertile, moist and less sandy than that of the outer coastal plain. Soils in this area contain large amounts of glauconite or greensand marl. In some areas the mineral is so abundant that the soil is dark green. Much of this region serves as the transportation corridor between New York and Philadelphia, complete with the accompanying development. Land not developed is cleared and devoted to agriculture. Fruit, vegetable, dairy and poultry farms dot the remaining open space, but these are disappearing at an alarming rate. As farms and fields are abandoned they become small havens of eastern cottontails, ring-necked pheasants, woodchucks, garter snakes and field sparrows.

As early as 1900 this area was reported to be only 15 percent wooded. For the most part it is only the wetter lowlands that contain extensive tracts of natural vegetation. Virgin forest has disappeared and the woodlands that remain are predominantly pine-oak on the drier, sandier soils, mixed-oak on the mesic uplands and hardwood swamp forests in the low-lying wet areas. Many southern species of plants, like sweet gum, willow oak, Spanish oak and persimmon, reach their northern limit on the inner coastal plain.

Hamilton-Trenton Marsh

PHOTO BY LAURIE PETTIGREW/NJDFW

Description

Located in densely developed Hamilton Township just south of Trenton, Hamilton-Trenton Marsh is the northernmost freshwater tidal marsh on the Delaware River. It contains a mixture of upland habitats, including deciduous woods and scrub-shrub, tidal and nontidal wetlands and open water. It links the Crosswicks, Delaware & Raritan and Delaware River greenways and contains the Trenton Marsh Natural Heritage Priority Site, considered one of the state's most significant natural areas.

Hamilton-Trenton Marsh has long been impacted by humans, starting with Native Americans some 6,000 years ago. In the mid-1800s the D&R Canal and Camden and Amboy railroads were constructed across the marsh. The marsh was bisected by several major highways and partially filled in to create landfill space.

In spite of these assaults on its integrity, Hamilton-Trenton Marsh serves as important habitat for over 1,000 species of plants and animals and provides recreational opportunities. The best way to experience this site is by boat, but walking the trails can be fruitful too.

Wildlife to Watch

Birding along any of the roads or trails is popular during spring migration. You may see yellow-throated vireos, black-and-white warblers, American redstarts and scarlet tanagers in the wooded areas along the bluffs and thrushes, tufted titmice and chickadees in the thickets of mountain laurel.

Great
▲ SITE ▲

At Spring Lake, walk west from the parking area around the wooded island or follow the path along the south edge of the lake. Look for mergansers and double-crested cormorants in the winter and cliff swallows, ospreys, green-winged teal, northern shoveler and wood ducks during the spring and summer. Scan the edges of the marsh areas and you are likely to see signs of muskrat, beaver, turtles and frogs. Look and listen for marsh wren, Virginia rail, sora, least bittern and pied-billed grebe. There is a scenic overlook from I-295 that offers a view of the river and marsh.

A healthy fishery exists here; species include carp, killifish, Johnny darter, alewife, shad and yellow perch. There are short-nosed sturgeon in the Delaware River. These fish support fish-eating animals like river otter, osprey, mergansers, cormorants, egrets and herons.

Audubon
IMPORTANT
BIRD AREAS

Trails

There are over 8 miles of walking trails and 11 miles of water trails at the park. The Outdoor Club of South Jersey hosts monthly canoe/kayak trips on the marsh. Call 609-259-3734 or go to www.marsh-friends.org and click the link for canoe and kayak trips.

Site Notes The park is open daily from dawn to dusk. Maps of the marsh and trails and detailed directions are available online at www.marsh-friends.org.

Size 1,250 acres

Directions From I-295 take exit 61A onto Arena Drive east. Turn right onto Woodside Avenue in 200 yds. Go four blocks to South Broad Street (US 206) and turn right. To Spring Lake: Follow South Broad Street to Sewell Avenue and follow to end. Turn left on dirt road into Roebling Park and downhill to Spring Lake. To Watson Woods: Follow South Broad Street to West Park Avenue. Turn left and travel to Westcott Street. Turn left onto Westcott Street then right into Roebling Park. Follow the road steeply downhill through the gate.

Nearest Town Hamilton

Ownership Mercer County Park Commission and NJ Department of Transportation

Contact 609-989-6559; www.nj.gov/counties/mercer/commissions/park/roebling_park.html

Delaware and Raritan Greenway: 609-924-4646, www.drgreenway.org

Friends of the Marsh: www.marsh-friends.org

Features trails, parking, interpretive signs, hiking, canoeing/kayaking

Great
▲ SITE ▲

Palmyra Cove

PHOTO BY LAURIE PETTIGREW/NJDFW

Description

Located at the base of the Tacony-Palmyra Bridge across the Delaware River from Philadelphia, this small urban park gives the impression of being removed from the hubbub of urban life. Palmyra Cove is still considered an active dredge spoil site, but the site hasn't been used in years and has reverted to woods and wetlands. This green diamond surrounded by concrete attracts an amazing 250-plus species of birds during the year—and unusual birds at that! This is the place to go to see that rare migrant. It also harbors over 300 species of plants, 49 fish varieties, 16 mammal species and 7 types of herptiles. The Environmental Discovery Center offers classrooms and an exhibit hall in a beautiful setting overlooking the river.

Wildlife to Watch

This is one of the most consistent places in the state to see yellow-bellied flycatcher, Philadelphia vireo and Lincoln's sparrow. Palmyra Cove also has nesting pied-billed grebe, least bittern, Acadian flycatcher, eastern wood-pewee, Baltimore oriole and Carolina chickadee. Peregrine falcons nest on the Tacony-Palmyra Bridge and frequently hunt at the park. Check out the Big Pit and surrounding area in early morning for a chance to see American bittern, red-headed woodpecker, golden-winged warbler, common moorhen, stilt sandpiper and black tern. Sparrows have included Lincoln's, LeConte's, clay-colored and Nelson's sharp-tailed. Listen for the burble of the marsh wren as you walk around the tidal cove. In winter, large numbers of waterfowl including American black duck, green-winged teal and northern pintail dabble in the cove while

Great
▲ SITE ▲

bufflehead, common goldeneye and common mergansers dive in the river. Scan the river for gulls. Such species as Iceland, glaucous and Bonaparte's have been spotted during migration. You are more likely to see mammal signs than actual mammals; look for tracks and scat along the trails and muddy banks.

Audubon
IMPORTANT
BIRD AREAS

Trails

There are 8 miles of trails that wind through the park along the Delaware River, past the dredge spoil pit and tidal cove, through woods and wetlands. A trail brochure is available at the Environmental Discovery Center.

Site Notes Stay on the trails to avoid stinging nettle and poison ivy. A birding checklist and map of the hot spots is available at the Environmental Discovery Center. Check one of the birding hotlines to find out what's being seen.

Size 250 acres

Directions Take NJ 73 north to the last traffic light before the Tacony-Palmyra Bridge Toll Plaza and turn right (corner of Souder Street and Route 73). Go two blocks to Temple Boulevard; turn left then make a right to the Toll Building parking lot, just before the Toll Plaza. Travel through the parking lot behind the Toll Building on the left, continue on the narrow local access road, and go under the bridge. The Environmental Discovery Center will be in front of you to the right. The parking area is to the left.

Nearest Town Palmyra

Ownership NJDEP Bureau of Tidelands Management

Contact 856-829-1900; www.palmyracove.org

Features hiking, restrooms, drinking water, interpretive center, interpretive programs, observation platform, trails, picnicking

Bonaparte's Gull PHOTO BY BOB CUNNINGHAM

Great
▲ SITE ▲

Garter Snake

Description

Hidden in the southwestern part of the state, Parvin State Park has a history as varied as its wildlife. The park once served as a station for the Civilian Conservation Corps (CCC) in the 1930s, as a summer camp for displaced Japanese workers during WWII and as a prisoner-of-war camp for German prisoners.

Situated on the edge of the New Jersey Pine Barrens, the forest covering is mostly oak-pine dominated forest with an open understory of low ericaceous shrubs like blueberry and huckleberry. In the lowlands along Muddy Run are hardwoods like red maple and black gum with Atlantic white cedar. The understory here is dense with sweet pepperbush and leatherleaf, which make the area attractive to many species of birds and insects. This site also contains the Parvin Lake Natural Heritage Priority Site, a significant New Jersey natural area.

Spring is a wonderful time to visit, with the bright colors and rich fragrances of blossoming dogwood, laurel, holly, magnolia and wild azalea. Thundergust Lake, Parvin Lake and Muddy Run provide habitat for waterfowl, turtles, frogs and snakes, but the attraction here is migrant songbirds. The best time to visit is April through mid-June during peak songbird migration. August and September can be productive too.

Wildlife to Watch

At least 136 species of birds travel through or reside in the park. Find white-tailed deer, white-footed mice and river otters. Frogs, salamanders, toads, turtles and nonvenomous snakes can be found along the lakeshores, in the swamp and along Muddy Run. Walk the trail through Parvin Natural Area to Muddy Run and chances are good you'll see and hear prothonotary warblers. Listen and look for white-eyed and red-eyed vireo, blue-gray gnatcatcher, gray catbird, wood thrush, yellow-billed cuckoo, Acadian flycatcher, common yellowthroat and Louisiana waterthrush. The upland woods should produce summer and scarlet tanager, Carolina wren, pine, prairie, hooded and blue-winged warbler, yellow-throated vireo, brown thrasher, ovenbird, wild turkey and, if you're lucky, broad-winged hawk. Listen for eastern screech-owl, barred owl and whip-poor-will at dusk.

Audubon
IMPORTANT
BIRD AREAS

Trails

Seven miles of trails includes the 1-mile-long Thundergust Lake Trail, the connecting Long Trail, which covers more than 5 miles around the perimeter of the park and the short Nature Trail. Trail guides are available at the office.

Site Notes Parvin State Park is open daily from dawn to dusk. The campground is open from March 1 to November 30.

Size 1,960 acres

Directions From exit 35 on New Jersey 55, take Garden Road toward Brotmanville. Travel 0.7 mile to Gershel Avenue. Turn left and, after 1.7 miles, turn right onto CR Route 540. Follow CR 540 for 2.4 miles to the park entrance and travel an additional 0.3 mile to reach the park office.

Nearest Town Centerton

Ownership NJDEP Division of Parks and Forestry

Contact 856-935-3218; www. njparksandforests.org

Features camping, picnicking, trails, hiking, biking, interpretive center, interpretive programs, boat launch, canoeing/kayaking, food, drinking water, restrooms

Carolina Wren PHOTO BY STEVE BYLAND

Great
▲ SITE ▲

Salem River

PHOTO BY LAURIE PETTIGREW/NJDFW

Description

Known locally as Mannington Marsh or Meadows, much of the marsh was impounded for agricultural purposes in the 1700s. The rest of the marsh is tidal and, as it is in the upper reaches of the Delaware estuary, it flows with brackish water. The Wildlife Management Area is made up of several old farms, and some of the walking trails follow former nursery roads. Look around for trees in unusual groupings. These are nursery stock that have grown wild and now provide valuable habitat for songbirds in migration.

Mannington Meadows sits amidst New Jersey's largest agricultural region and is surrounded by farmland and rural development. The meadow contains one of the largest wild rice stands in New Jersey; the Mannington Meadows Natural Heritage Priority Macrosite is one of southern New Jersey's most important stopover sites for migratory waterfowl and shorebirds.

Wildlife to Watch

Turn down the dirt lane from NJ 45 just north of the meadow at the WMA sign. Stop at the first pull-off and walk toward the meadow to an observation tower set high above the marsh. Drive further down the dirt lane to a second, larger parking area and a lower elevated platform at the edge of the marsh.

Fall and winter birding is excellent when the pickerelweed, spatterdock and American lotus die down, making it easier to see the rafts of ducks. And spring migration is amazing here. Look for northern pintails, gadwalls, American wigeon, American black duck, greater scaup, and green-winged teal. Thousands of Canada geese and snow geese feed in the nearby farm fields during the fall and winter. Nesting birds include American coots, mute swans and an abundance of red-winged blackbirds. Wading birds like cattle, snowy and great egret, great blue, little blue and tri-colored heron, and black-crowned night heron feed in the marsh as do bald eagle and osprey. Sandpipers utilize the mud flats. Walk along the many old roads during spring and fall migration to look for warblers, vireos, thrushes and other songbirds. Summer residents include yellow warblers, gray catbird, white-eyed vireo, yellow-billed cuckoo, prairie warbler and common yellowthroats. Muskrat and beaver are common as are groundhog, gray squirrel, red fox and coyote.

You can drive along the northern side of the meadow to view both the tidal and non-tidal sections. There is no parking and fast traffic on NJ 45 and CR 540, but there are views from Nimrod Road and Sunset Drive. A dirt lane on the left just south of Nimrod Road on CR 540 offers a short walk along the marsh edge. Pull into the lane and park to the side.

Audubon
IMPORTANT
BIRD AREAS

Trails

There are no marked trails but many old roads and trails are suitable for walking. Trails leave from the parking area on NJ 45.

Site Notes	Salem River WMA is a natural area with no facilities. Salem River WMA is open for hunting during prescribed seasons.
Size	1,121 acres
Directions	From US Highway 40 and NJ 45, drive 4.3 miles south on NJ 45 to WMA sign on the right (west) side of the road. Pull in to park. Or, for other views of the marsh, continue 1.8 miles south on NJ 45 to first right turn (Bypass Road). Go 0.1 mile and turn right onto CR 620. Travel 1.6 miles to the overlook. To continue from the overlook, turn left onto Nimrod Road and travel 1.8 miles to CR 540. Turn left again and travel 1.8 miles back to NJ 45, stopping for views along the way. Please obey posted signs in these locations; they are located outside the WMA.
Nearest Town	Salem
Ownership	NJDEP Division of Fish, Game and Wildlife
Contact	856-785-0455, www.njfishandwildlife.com
Features	parking, hiking

LOWER DELAWARE RIVER ■ *Salem River Wildlife Management Area*

Great
▲ SITE ▲

LOWER DELAWARE RIVER ■ Supawna Meadows National Wildlife Refuge/Fort Mott State Park

Supawna Meadows National Wildlife Refuge

Description

Fort Mott State Park is located on the banks of the Delaware River in the upper reaches of the estuary. Built as part of a coastal defense system in the late 1800s, much of the fort remains intact today. In summer visitors can take a ferry ride to nearby Fort Delaware on Peapatch Island and Fort Dupont in Delaware City and view colonies of wading birds and their rookeries on Peapatch Island.

Nearby Supawna Meadows National Wildlife Refuge encompasses over 3,000 acres of brackish tidal marsh, grasslands, forest and forested wetland. It provides critical habitat for migrating, wintering and breeding birds and serves as a nursery for fish and shellfish.

Wildlife to Watch

Scan the river from the battlements at Fort Mott for gulls, ducks and geese, particularly in winter. Large flocks of American robins congregate on the lawn in late winter. Take a ride on the ferry to Peapatch Island for a chance to see nine species of herons and egrets. Walk the woodland trails at dawn or dusk and you might catch a glimpse of a red fox, Virginia opossum or striped skunk.

Spring and fall migration bring warblers, sparrows, sandpipers, wading birds and waterfowl. Walk the Forest Habitat Trail in spring and hear spring peepers and leopard frogs and see wood ducks in the wetlands. Take the grassland trail and look for eastern kingbirds, eastern bluebirds and eastern meadowlark. From the observation platform, scan the marsh for little blue and tri-colored herons. Many threatened or endangered species nest on the refuge including osprey, bald eagle, American kestrel, northern harrier, king rail and barn

Great
▲ SITE ▲

owl. Fall migration begins in August with the staging of thousands of tree swallows that gather to feed on insects. Look for American kestrels hunting from roadside wires in September and October. Northern pintails, mallards and American black ducks winter in the marsh. The most common mammals include white-tailed deer, muskrat, red fox, eastern cottontail and groundhog.

Audubon
IMPORTANT
BIRD AREAS

Trails

There is a short, universally accessible interpretive nature trail in Fort Mott State Park. Trails on the refuge provide easy walking through varied habitats with good viewing opportunities. The 1.25-mile Grassland Trail starts from the parking area on Lighthouse Road and is accessible to the platform. The 1.3-mile Forest Habitat Loop Trail begins at the parking area on Christmas Tree Lane. A designated boat trail is reached from the Salem River.

Site Notes	Go to www.threeforts.com/sched.html to check the ferry schedule as hours are not always regular. There are no facilities at Supawna Meadow NWR at this time, although there are facilities at Ft. Mott. Go to www.fws.gov/northeast/nj/spm.htm for a downloadable brochure.
Size	Fort Mott: 104 acres
	Supawna Meadow: 3,000 acres
Directions	Take I-295 to exit 1C on CR 551. Follow CR 551 to its end at NJ 49. Turn left onto NJ 49 east. Go 1 mile to first right onto Lighthouse Road. Turn right and take Lighthouse Road to parking area on left. Continue straight to Fort Mott Road for Fort Mott State Park. Bear left onto Fort Mott Road and travel 1 mile to park entrance on right.
Nearest Town	Salem
Ownership	Fort Mott State Park: NJDEP Division of Parks and Forestry
	Supawna Meadows: US Fish and Wildlife Service
Contact	Fort Mott: 856-935-3218; www.njparksandforests.org
	Supawna Meadow: 609-463-0994; www.fws.gov/northeast/nj/spm.htm
Features	Coastal Heritage Trail site, restrooms, picnicking, trails, drinking water, hiking, parking, interpretive signs

Fox Sparrow   *PHOTO BY BOB CUNNINGHAM*

Great
▲ SITE ▲

LOWER DELAWARE RIVER ■ *Supawna Meadows National Wildlife Refuge/Fort Mott State Park*

Abbotts Meadow Wildlife Management Area/PSEG Alloway Creek Watershed Wetland Restoration Site

Description

Abbotts Meadow Wildlife Management Area is known for its grassland and early-successional birds. The ecotone formed at the edge of the saltmarsh is the perfect habitat for a multitude of species as it bumps up against farm fields interspersed with hedgerows and wooded copses. The several species of sparrows you are likely to see in the pastures give the area an outstanding reputation for birding.

Wildlife to Watch

Park in either of the PSEG parking areas at the end of Money Island Road and walk the road scanning the hedgerows to look for white-crowned and white-throated sparrow, dickcissel, pipits, meadowlark, bobolink and yellow-breasted chat. Take the footpath at the end of Money Island Road along the dike to the observation platform or walk the loop trail through the saltmarsh. The hummocks or small islands you'll cross along the way provide important feeding and resting sites for migrating birds, raptors and wintering owls. Look for northern harrier, egrets, herons and rails. The high tension wires from the power plant offer roosting places for black vultures, turkey vultures and ospreys nesting in the area.

Trails

A short trail at the end of Money Island Road leads to an observation platform, and a longer loop trail (complete with a platform) leaves the first parking area to wind along a creek and over hummock islands. There are additional parking areas with access to fields and unmarked trails along Fort Elfsborg Road and Abbotts Farm Road.

Site Notes: Abbots Meadow WMA is a natural area with no facilities and is open for hunting during prescribed seasons.

Size: 1,011 acres

Directions: Take NJ 49 east for 0.7 mile from its intersection with NJ 45 to CR 658. Turn right onto CR 658 (Hancock's Bridge Road) at the sign for Hancock's Bridge. Travel approximately 3 miles and turn right onto CR 624 (Fort Elfsborg Road). Proceed for 2 miles to Money Island Road and turn left. Proceed to either parking area.

Nearest Town: Salem

Ownership: NJDEP Division of Fish, Game and Wildlife; Public Service Electric & Gas

Contact: NJDEP: 856-785-0455; www.njfishandwildlife.com; Public Service Electric & Gas: 888-MARSHES; www.pseg.com/environment2008/estuary/overview.jsp

Features: observation platform, trails, parking

Camden County Parks

Description

Maria Barnaby Greenwald Memorial and Pennypacker Parks form a greenway along the Cooper River through this densely developed suburban neighborhood. Both parks are rich in history as well as wildlife. The remains of the first complete dinosaur skeleton were unearthed in 1858 in an area which is now part of the park. *Hadrosaurus foulkii* is now the New Jersey State Dinosaur. These parks act like a beacon of green, attracting migrating birds looking for a place to feed and rest. The 150-acre Berlin Park in the City of Berlin contains a wonderful stand of mature deciduous trees that attract migrant songbirds from April through mid-June.

Wildlife to Watch

At Greenwald Memorial Park, which lies within Pennypacker Park, you can hike or bike for more than a mile along the Cooper River. Early morning is the best time to see birds here, especially during the spring migration when the trees are alive with warblers and other songbirds but are not yet fully leafed out. During the summer visit Hopkins Pond and the surrounding mature hardwood forest (south on NJ 41 to right on Hopkins Lane) for glimpses of herons, osprey, turtles, raccoons and opossums. Vireos, warblers, orioles, scarlet tanagers and rose-breasted grosbeaks are attracted to the insects feeding on flowering deciduous trees in Berlin Park.

Trails

A 1.8-mile Watchable Wildlife Trail winds through the more natural Haddonfield section of the Pennypacker Park, and a 1.2-mile bike path runs its length. Visit the 0.6-mile Natural History Trail at Hopkins Pond. Brochures are available at the Park Administration building and at locations along the trail. Berlin Park offers 5 miles of hiking trails running through lowland woods along the Great Egg Harbor River.

Site Notes: Camden County Parks are open daily.

Size: Greenwald Memorial Park: 47 acres, Pennypacker Park: 32 acres, Berlin Park:151 acres

Directions: Greenwald Memorial Park: From NJ 70 in Cherry Hill, take NJ 41 south for 0.9 mile. Turn right onto Park Boulevard and park in any designated parking area.

Berlin Park: From NJ 30 (Whitehorse Pike) in Berlin, go south on Broad Street for three blocks. Park entrance is straight ahead.

Nearest Town: Cherry Hill, Haddonfield, Berlin

Ownership: Camden County Park System

Contact: 609-795-7275;
www.camdencounty.com/government/offices/parks/parks.html

Features: trails, hiking, parking, biking, picnicking

LOWER DELAWARE RIVER ■ Other Sites

Other sites

201

Description

Rancocas Nature Center sits north of Rancocas Creek and adjacent to Rancocas State Park in a 130-year-old farmhouse. The farmhouse has been turned into a nature center by the New Jersey Audubon Society and houses a museum, bookshop and classroom. Displays interpret the natural history of New Jersey and the Rancocas Watershed. Live reptiles and hands-on objects add to the learning experience.

A variety of ecological communities is protected at this reserve, including old fields and thickets, conifer plantations, upland oak-pine and floodplain forests and a freshwater tidal marsh along the Rancocas Creek. These varied communities support a diverse population of plants, animals and fungi, making the Rancocas Nature Center an ideal destination for anyone who wants to study nature.

Wildlife to Watch

Self-guided trails radiate out from the nature center into the adjoining parkland. Birding is best in May, but over 160 species of birds live in the area year-round. Red-tailed hawks and mammals such as white-tailed deer, red foxes and muskrats are usually visible year-round. Wood ducks nest around the marshes from April to September, and Canada geese and other waterfowl are usually present in February and March. Spring migration brings warblers, thrushes, vireos and sparrows. Don't miss the Children's Garden or the Butterfly and Hummingbird Garden.

Trails

Four trails (red, blue, yellow and orange) wind through the various habitats. All are less than 1 mile long and cover easy terrain. A trail guide and map are available online and offer detailed information on trail length, difficulty, highlights and special notes.

Site Notes: The NJAS Nature Center is open Tuesday through Sunday. Closed Monday and holidays. The Powhatan Indians host an annual festival. Call 609-261-2495 for information.

Size: 120 acres

Directions: From I-295, take the Westhampton exit 45A. Travel east on CR 626 (Rancocas Road) for 1.7 miles to the entrance on the right.

Nearest Town: Mount Holly

Ownership: New Jersey Audubon Society

Contact: 609-261-2495; www.njaudubon.org

Features: trails, parking, interpretive center, interpretive signage, interpretive programs, drinking water, restrooms

LOWER DELAWARE RIVER ■ Other Sites

Other sites

Chipping Sparrow

Wild Turkey

LOWER DELAWARE RIVER ■ *Other Sites*

Other sites

Cape May-Delaware Bay

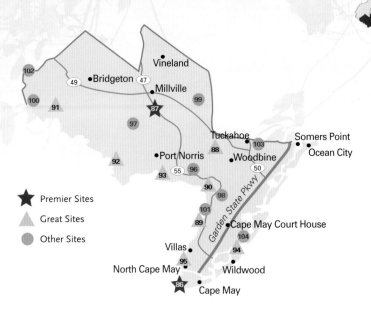

★ Premier Sites

🔺 Great Sites

⬤ Other Sites

View uncommon plants and rare birds

Sandy and flat, the Cape May-Delaware Bay Region is part of the outer coastal plain. Bordered on the east by the Atlantic Ocean and on the west by Delaware Bay, the region boasts some of the best bird watching in the state. The funnel-like shape of the Cape May Peninsula acts to concentrate birds as they migrate down the Atlantic coast. Many species of birds rest and refuel here before and after crossing the Delaware Bay during spring and fall migration. Breeding birds are abundant and include many endangered species such as the bald eagle and the black rail.

Because federal and state agencies and nonprofit conservation organizations own a large percentage of the land, the Delaware Bayshore has the lowest population density in New Jersey. The high concentration of rare and endangered plants and animals in this area is due to this lack of development. In fact, the endangered tiger salamander and the southern gray treefrog live only in this region in New Jersey.

One of the few places in the world where you can find sensitive joint vetch, a twining marsh plant, is along the wild and scenic Maurice River. The state's largest native stands of wild rice grow along the river banks and Atlantic white cedars line the stream corridors and bogs. The large tracts of southern hardwood and pine-oak forests covering the region's interior provide some of the best habitat in the state for forest-dependent species like the barred owl, red-shouldered hawk and the hundreds of songbirds that nest here and winter in the tropics.

Salt marshes border the region, forming where shallow ocean or bay waters meet gently sloping, sheltered coastlines. This occurs on the east coast behind barrier islands and on the west coast in sheltered bay coves. The salt marsh acts as a "breadbasket," producing nearly 10 tons of organic matter per acre per year. This organic matter forms the basis of a food web that benefits species living in the salt marsh and those living outside of it too, including humans. Fresh food and nutrients flow into tidal creeks with the tides twice daily, providing ample food for the creatures that live in or near the marsh.

This is an agricultural area as well, producing lettuce, peppers, tomatoes, cabbages and soybeans. Large wholesale nurseries and smaller garden centers supplement the region's agriculture, giving credence to New Jersey's nickname, "The Garden State." Traditional local industries in the past included boat building, fishing and oystering. In the early 1900s, Bivalve was the oyster capital of the world. The fish and shellfish industries have declined since the 1950s, but the state's remnant oyster fleet still sits at the docks in the towns of Bivalve and Shellpile. Major industries in the area today are sand mining and glass manufacturing. Sand mining operations leave large, deep lakes often surrounded by sandy beaches, which are used by beach-nesting birds.

Fortunately, much of this region has retained its rural flavor. The abundance of federal, state and nonprofit lands has played an important role in maintaining the ecological integrity of this region.

New Jersey's Artificial Reef Program

New Jersey's Artificial Reef Program began in 1984. Since that time, 15 artificial reefs have been constructed along New Jersey's 127 miles of coast. Artificial reefs have been placed so that at least one reef site is within easy reach of 12 of New Jersey's major inlets.

The reefs, constructed by sinking objects like ships, tug boats, barges, subway cars, and concrete rubble, create structure on New Jersey's mostly flat, sandy ocean floor. Blue mussels, barnacles and other marine invertebrates colonize the reef structures providing food, shelter and hiding places for fish and other marine creatures including sea bass, blackfish, porgy and lobster. Artificial reefs provide anglers and scuba divers with a multitude of recreational and viewing opportunities.

For more information and the latitude/longitude coordinates of each reef go to www.njfishandwildlife.com/artreef.htm

Rockland County Artifical Reef

PHOTO BY HERB SEGARS

Northern Gannet

PHOTO BY BOB CUNNINGHAM

Description

Location, location, location is what makes Cape May a world-renowned birding hot spot. While the spring migration is impressive, the fall migration is downright phenomenal; summer and winter are merely excellent. Because of migratory patterns and geology, something is always migrating through Cape May. Spring migration can begin as early as mid-February and fall migration can begin in August. Often there are birds moving north as others are moving south.

Birds utilize wind currents to help minimize energy consumption during migration. Northern breeding birds tend to fly east and south during fall migration, thus hitting the Atlantic coast. As most birds are reluctant to fly over large bodies of water, most continue south. The Cape May Peninsula serves as a pinch point between the Atlantic Ocean and Delaware Bay, a nearly 10-mile journey over open water from Cape May to Cape Henlopen. Birds and insects often stack up on the Cape waiting for favorable wind conditions before venturing south or heading up the Delaware Bayshore to seek a way to avoid a water crossing. Conversely, birds moving north in the spring often stop to rest and feed in Cape May after making the flight across the bay. The remaining undeveloped habitat on this highly developed peninsula provides critical resting and feeding spots for migrating birds as they continue their grueling journey. The best birding occurs after a cold front in the fall and with a warm front in the spring, as birds migrate along the edges of these air masses. This viewing area wraps around the tip of the peninsula and includes Cape May Point State Park, Cape May Migratory Refuge and Higbee Beach Wildlife Management Area

Premier
★ SITE ★

Wildlife to Watch

The 157-foot-tall Cape May Lighthouse at Cape May Point State Park marks land's end for birds and mariners. On good flight days the lighthouse serves as a sky-high tower from which to catch a bird's eye view of the cape, the Atlantic Ocean and Delaware Bay. It also serves as a vantage point from which to catch an extraordinary look at migrating raptors from above. Nearby, the "hawk watch," as the park's multi-level observation platform is known, is the heart and soul of Cape May birding in the fall. The platform faces northeast over a freshwater pond and marsh, with the Atlantic Ocean off to the right and additional ponds, bayberry thickets and copses of woods to the left. A perch on the platform provides a panoramic view so chock-full of birds you won't know which way to point your binoculars. Sparrows and finches feed in the bushes at the base of the platform. Waterfowl, herons, terns, gulls, egrets and shorebirds feed in the pond and marsh, including an impressive array of sandpiper species. Pelagic birds and an occasional pod of bottlenose dolphins may be seen just off the beach, monarch and buckeye butterflies flutter past as dragonflies dart after wasps and beetles and merlin perform aerobatic maneuvers chasing startled sandpipers from the mudflats while kettles of raptors soar high overhead.

Beginning in September and extending through December, tens of thousands of raptors, including bald eagle, peregrine falcon, osprey, goshawk, Cooper's hawk,

Least Tern

PHOTO BY CONSTANCE CAMPANELLA

sharp-shinned hawk and various species of owls pass the platform on the point. It is not uncommon to see Mississippi kites or even the occasional swallow-tailed kite. Birding is good here at all times of the year. Walk the trails and boardwalk through the natural area where several benches, platforms and a photo blind provide additional places to stroll or sit and watch the show unfurl.

The Cape May Migratory Bird Refuge, owned by The Nature Conservancy since 1981, is an internationally significant coastal wetland situated along the Atlantic Flyway. A diversity of habitats makes this one of the most important migratory stopovers in the world for birds of prey, shorebirds, songbirds and waterfowl, as well as an important breeding area for both rare and common birds. About 60,000 raptors and over a million seabirds migrate through this area each year, taking advantage of the refuge's ocean beach, primary and secondary dunes, fresh and brackish water marshes, maritime forest, thickets, wetland meadows and fields. A massive, multimillion-dollar restoration completed in 2007 was the result of a partnership between the U.S. Army Corps of Engineers, the New Jersey Department of Environmental Protection and The Nature Conservancy's New Jersey Chapter. The project included invasive species removal and control, nearly 2 miles of beach replenishment and dune creation and enhancement. A 4-acre pond behind the dune system is specifically designed as foraging and nesting habitat for piping plovers and least terns. A 60-foot-wide channel was created that runs through the preserve and feeds three levees, each with a water control structure that allows the Conservancy to control water levels throughout the preserve.

Higbee Beach Wildlife Management Area, which is located just around the point on the bayfront, is managed specifically for migratory wildlife. Visitors are often rewarded with glimpses of a hundred or more species of migrating songbirds and hawks. Higbee contains the last coastal dune forest on the Delaware Bay. In addition to coastal dune forest, there are old fields, scrub/shrub thickets, mixed-deciduous woods and wooded wetlands, two small freshwater ponds, brackish tidal wetlands, a mile of beachfront and acres of coastal grasslands. The shrub thickets, woods and fields teem with songbirds gleaning insects, seeds and fruits to fuel their migration, while hawks performing aerial acrobatics pursue those same songbirds. This scenario is repeated thousands of times everywhere on the cape where housing and commercial development has not replaced natural habitats. Birds are not the only migrants to pass through Cape May. Butterflies, particularly monarchs, nectar on the goldenrod in the fields and dunes. If you walk the beach, keep an eye open for dolphins swimming along the coast. Also, listen for Cope's gray treefrog and look for eastern box turtles. Endangered tiger salamanders breed here in late winter.

Audubon
IMPORTANT
BIRD AREAS

Premier
★ SITE ★

Trails

A large portion of Cape May Point State Park is a designated Natural Area and has over three miles of trails and boardwalks. There is universal access to the hawk watch platform, trails and beach from the parking lot. A 0.5-mile, self-guided nature trail is barrier-free. The Cape May Migratory Bird Refuge boasts a 1.3-mile walking trail over level terrain and a spectacular viewing platform with a 360-degree view of the refuge and across Delaware Bay; on a clear day it's possible to see Delaware's Cape Henlopen.

Higbee Beach WMA has several miles of marked trails; trail surfaces include grass, sand and mowed paths. There are three observation platforms (near the main parking area at the end of New England Road) overlooking various habitats. Site and trail maps can be downloaded from the Division of Fish and Wildlife's website.

Site Notes   Cape May Point State Park: The park is open seven days a week from dawn to dusk. The visitor center is open daily. Nature programs are offered on weekends.

Cape May Migratory Bird Refuge: The refuge is open seven days a week from dawn to dusk. A visitor pass is required and is available on site for a small fee.

Higbee Beach WMA: Higbee Beach is open for hunting during certain prescribed seasons.

New Jersey Audubon Society's Cape May Bird Observatory volunteers and staff also provide informative programs at Cape May Point State Park for visitors throughout the fall and lead bird walks at Higbee Beach in spring and fall. Call 609-861-0700 or go to www.njaudubon.org or www.birdcapemay.org for information.

Size   Cape May Point State Park: 235 acres

Cape May Migratory Bird Refuge: 219 acres

Higbee Beach WMA: 1,090 acres

Directions   Cape May Point State Park: Continue straight at the end of the Garden State Parkway onto US 109 south, which becomes Lafayette Street (CR 633) in 0.4 mile. Continue on Lafayette Street for 1.8 miles through Cape May. Turn right onto Jackson Street (CR 633) and travel 0.1 mile and bear left onto West Perry Street (CR 633). Go 0.3 mile to traffic light. Continue straight onto Sunset Boulevard (CR 606). Go 2.5 miles to Lighthouse Avenue. Turn left and go 1.0 mile to park entrance on the left.

Cape May Migratory Refuge: Follow the above directions onto Sunset Boulevard (CR 606). Go 1 mile to refuge entrance on left.

Higbee Beach WMA: Follow above directions onto Sunset Boulevard (CR 606). Travel 2.8 miles to parking area on the right just before the end of Sunset Boulevard. Or, take Sunset Boulevard (CR 606) for 0.3 mile and turn right onto Bayshore Road (CR 607). Go 1.5 miles to New England Road (CR 641). Turn left and go 0.25 mile to first parking area on left. Continue to the end of New England Road for main parking area.

Nearest Town Cape May Point

Ownership Cape May Point State Park: NJDEP Division of Parks and Forestry

Cape May Migratory Bird Refuge: The Nature Conservancy

Higbee Beach WMA: NJDEP Division of Fish and Wildlife

Contact Cape May Point State Park: NJDEP Division of Parks and Forestry: 609-884-2159; www.njparksandforests.org

Cape May Migratory Bird Refuge: The Nature Conservancy: 609-861-0600; www.nature.org/newjersey

Higbee Beach WMA: NJDEP Division of Fish and Wildlife: 856-785-0455; www.njfishandwildlife.com

Features parking, restrooms, barrier-free, picnicking, trails, hiking, biking, interpretive programs, visitor center, interpretive signage, observation platform, photo blind, scenic overlook, drinking water

Blue-winged Teal

PHOTO BY STEVE BYLAND

Premier
★ SITE ★

Photo by Damon Noe

Bald Eagle

PHOTO BY JIM MALLMAN

Description

This long, linear viewing area spans both sides of the river and includes stops at Fowser Municipal Boat Ramp, Harold N. Peek Preserve, Mauricetown Municipal Park, PSEG Commercial Township Salt Hay Farm Wetland Restoration Site and Maurice River Bluffs. The Maurice River and its tributaries form a pristine coastal river system that flows through the Pine Barrens Region of the Outer Coastal Plain to the Delaware Bay. Its clean waters and wetland habitats are vitally important to shorebirds, songbirds, waterfowl, raptors, rails, fish, reptiles and amphibians. Habitats include stands of Atlantic white cedar, hardwood swamps, freshwater streams, fresh and brackish water tidal rivers, mud flats and fresh, brackish and salt water marsh. Note the differences in habitats as you move from the upper, fresher region of the river system to its lower, saltier confluence with Delaware Bay.

This system contains nationally and internationally important resources. It supports New Jersey's largest stand of wild rice and has the largest global population of sensitive joint vetch. It serves as a critical link between the Pinelands National Reserve and the Delaware Estuary. Fifteen of New Jersey's 25 endangered and threatened birds breed within this river system. The excellent water quality and undisturbed nature of the area are reflected in the diversity of species that call this area home. The state's largest and perhaps only population of the northern scarlet snake is found here along with northern pine snake, corn snake and Cope's gray treefrog.

Thousands of years before European settlers arrived, Native Americans used the resources of the river. Today the Maurice River supports such industries as

CAPE MAY-DELAWARE BAY ■ *Maurice River Viewing Areas*

Premier
★ SITE ★

commercial crabbing, eeling, net fishing and oystering, activities that are dependent upon the river's ecological integrity. The A.J. Meerwald, a restored 1928 oyster schooner and New Jersey's official Tall Ship, serves as a floating classroom.

The river is also a place where thousands of people pursue recreational activities such as pleasure boating, canoeing, kayaking, wildlife watching, fishing and hunting. The best way to experience the river is from the river. Many local non-profit organizations offer boating trips on the river from spring through fall. There are also several locations where a small motor boat, canoe or kayak can be launched to enjoy a day on the river.

Wildlife to Watch

Start at Fowser Municipal Boat Ramp for a quick scan of the upper river for bald eagle, belted kingfisher, American black duck, mallard, wood duck and Canada geese. In the spring and summer the river comes alive with the herring run.

Drive the short distance to Natural Lands Trust's Harold N. Peek Preserve for views of the wild rice marsh from one of its observation areas. Look for northern harrier, bank swallow, Forster's and least tern, muskrat, mink, raccoon, red-winged blackbird, marsh wren, egrets, herons, rails and waterfowl. This wild rice marsh attracts thousands of wintering waterfowl each year. Migrating shad and striped bass provide food for bald eagle and osprey. Trails lead through various habitats including pine forest, Atlantic white cedar swamp and hardwood swamp. Springtime brings wildflowers and an array of songbirds including prothonotary,

Osprey

Premier
★ SITE ★

worm-eating, yellow, prairie and pine warblers, Baltimore and orchard oriole, gray catbird and common yellowthroat.

Make a quick stop at the Mauricetown Municipal Park in spring or summer to see the purple martin colony. In August the vast phragmites-infested marsh to the north of the bridge serves as New Jersey's largest staging area for swallows. Thousands of swallows swarm above the river feeding on the plentitude of hatching insects. Mauricetown hosts the Purple Martin Festival in August to celebrate this phenomenon and the Winter Eagle Festival in February to celebrate the success of the state's bald eagle recovery program.

PSEG's Commercial Township Restoration site, managed by The Nature Conservancy, reflects the estuarine nature of the lower river. This vast area of restored salt marsh bordered by uplands was previously diked to grow salt hay. Since being restored to tide, this area is popular with waterfowl, shorebirds, gulls, terns, raptors and wading birds. The mouth of the river is a critical staging area for migratory shorebirds, and hundreds of thousands of snow geese and rafts of scoters, scaup, bufflehead and cormorants winter on these marshes. Short-eared owl, northern harrier and bald eagle are common.

Work your way north to the last stop, the 40-plus-foot-tall Maurice River Bluffs. The Nature Conservancy established the Maurice River Bluffs Nature Preserve as important stopover habitat for migrating and breeding birds, including songbirds, waterfowl and raptors. The preserve also hosts freshwater ponds and unique plant communities. The site contains an excellent example of contiguous wild rice marshes. The view from the bluffs is magnificent, as is the view from the bench on the dock on the river.

Trails

There are a number of trails at the Peek Preserve leading through the various habitats. Trails cover mostly flat terrain over dirt, gravel or boardwalk. The PSEG site features a level, accessible walking/biking trail and three observation platforms. Maurice River Bluffs Preserve offers a loop trail system with trails ranging from 1 to 4 miles long over easy to moderate terrain on dirt surfaces.

Site Notes Peek Preserve: Visitors are welcome to park at the main gate (don't block the gate) and walk in when staff are not present. Call or check online for event schedule. No pets please.

Maurice River Bluffs: The preserve is open seven days a week from dawn to dusk. No pets please. The Nature Conservancy offers guided tours throughout the year. Call or check online for event schedule.

Additional programs are offered by The Bayshore Discovery Project (www.ajmeerwald.org) and Citizens United to Protect the Maurice River and its Tributaries (www.ajmeerwald.org; www.cumauriceriver.org).

Premier
★ SITE ★

Size Harold N. Peek Preserve: 252 acres

Maurice River Bluffs Nature Preserve: 550 acres

Public Service Enterprise Group: 4,171 acres

Directions From exit 24 on NJ 55 take NJ 49 north to NJ 47. Take NJ 47 south for 1 mile. Turn right (west) on Fowser Road and travel to parking area.

Harold N. Peek Preserve: Continue south on NJ 47 for 0.4 mile to Peek Preserve entrance on the right (look sharp, it's easy to miss).

Mauricetown Municipal Park: Continue south on NJ 47 for approximately 7 miles (bear right onto NJ47 not left onto NJ 347) to CR 670. Turn right and travel 1 mile over the Maurice River Causeway Bridge to blinker light. Turn left onto Front Street. Travel 0.2 mile to Highland Street and turn left. Drive to parking area on the right.

PSEG Restoration Site: Turn onto Highland Avenue (CR 676) and continue straight for 1 mile. Turn left at blinker light onto CR 649 (North Avenue). Travel approximately 2.5 miles to "T" intersection with CR 553 in Port Norris. Turn right onto CR 553 and travel 0.1 mile to High Street (CR 631). Turn left and go 0.4 mile to parking area on the right, across the street from the Bayshore Discovery Project.

Maurice River Bluffs Preserve: Return to CR 649 (North Avenue). Remain on CR 649 until it intersects CR 670 (approximately 3.0 miles). Turn left onto CR 670 (Buckshutem Road) and travel west for 4.0 miles. Bear right onto CR 627 (Silver Run Road) and travel 1.0 mile to preserve entrance on the right.

Nearest Town Millville

Ownership Fowser Municipal Boat Ramp: City of Millville

Harold N. Peek Preserve: Natural Lands Trust

Maurice River Bluffs Nature Preserve: The Nature Conservancy

Public Service Enterprise Group

Contact Fowser Municipal Boat Ramp: 609-825-7000

Harold N. Peek Preserve: 856-825-9952

Maurice River Bluffs Nature Preserve: 609-861-0600; www.nature.org/newjersey

Public Service Enterprise Group: 1-888-MARSHES; www.pseg.com/environment2008/estuary/overview.jsp

Features trails, hiking, canoeing/kayaking, observation platforms, scenic overlooks, interpretive programs, interpretive signs, boat launch, parking, picnicking, photo blind, checklist

Premier
★ SITE ★

Willet

PHOTO BY BOB CUNNINGHAM

Tree Swallow

PHOTO BY STEVE BYLAND

Premier
★ SITE ★

Belleplain State Forest

PHOTO BY LAURIE PETTIGREW/NJDFW

Description

Belleplain State Forest, one of New Jersey's oldest state forests, was established in 1928 for recreation, wildlife management, timber production and water conservation. Belleplain lies within the Pinelands National Reserve and offers a variety of habitats, including Atlantic white cedar swamp, mixed-hardwood swamp, shallow ponds and lakes, streams and pine-oak forest, and their associated wildlife. A largely unfragmented second-growth forest, Belleplain is the centerpiece of a 150,000-acre public land corridor that stretches from the Atlantic Coast to Delaware Bay and provides critical habitat for species requiring large territories of unbroken forest. The spring and fall migration of songbirds through Belleplain is enough to make the wildlife enthusiast go weak in the knees.

Wildlife to Watch

At its best in spring and early summer, birders are realizing Belleplain is also a good location in fall. There are consistently good finds of Kentucky, hooded, black-throated blue and green, worm-eating, northern parula, prothonotary, yellow-throated, pine, prairie, black-and-white and blue-winged warblers, American redstart, scarlet and summer tanagers, Baltimore and orchard orioles, yellow-billed cuckoo, Louisiana and northern waterthrush, red-eyed, white-eyed and yellow-throated vireos, eastern wood-pewee, Acadian and great-crested flycatchers, white-breasted nuthatch, red-headed, red-bellied, downy and hairy woodpeckers, wood thrush, brown thrasher and gray catbird. Many of these species breed here and can be seen through the summer.

Great
▲ SITE ▲

Fall brings the reverse and includes sparrows and raptors. Winter can be good for a variety of sparrows, pine siskin, purple finch and American goldfinch. Look for Hessel's hairstreak butterfly in the many Atlantic white cedar bogs.

Oak leaves decay slowly because of the tannin in their cells, leaving a thick batting of leaves. Small rodents, reptiles and amphibians tunnel under these leaves and use them to find food and stay warm or cool. Such species include spotted and marbled salamanders, five-lined skinks, eastern box turtles and red-backed voles. In some areas dead trees are left standing to provide vertical habitat diversity. Wildlife use these trees for nesting, feeding and perching. Look for cavity dwellers like flying squirrels, raccoons, Virginia opossums, red-headed and red-bellied woodpeckers and tufted titmice.

Trails

The forest has miles of marked trails and unimproved roads suitable for hiking, horseback riding, cross-country skiing and wildlife-watching. Walk the 1.5-mile, self-guided trail around Lake Nummy or the 6.5-mile East Creek Trail connecting to East Creek Pond. Trail guides are available at the park office.

Site Notes Belleplain is open seven days a week. The visitor center is open daily. Maps and trail guides are available at the office. Belleplain is open for hunting during prescribed seasons.

Size 21,320 acres

Directions From NJ 55 continue straight on NJ 47 to NJ 347, approximately 3.0 miles. Bear left onto NJ 347 and travel 2.5 miles to CR 550. Turn left and follow CR 550 (turn right at Woodbine Avenue) for approximately 5.0 miles to the state forest entrance on the right.

Nearest Town Woodbine

Ownership NJDEP Division of Parks and Forestry

Contact 609-861-2404; www. njparksandforests.org

Features visitor center, interpretive center, interpretive programs, trails, parking, restrooms, picnicking, camping, hiking, bicycling, horseback riding, canoeing/kayaking, entry fee (seasonal)

Hooded Warbler   PHOTO BY BOB CUNNINGHAM

Great
▲ SITE ▲

Cape May National Wildlife Refuge

PHOTO BY DAMON NOE

Description

Cape May National Wildlife Refuge provides critical habitat to a wide variety of migratory birds and other wildlife. Its value for the protection of migratory birds and their habitat will continue to grow as wildlife habitat along the Jersey Shore is depleted.

Three separate divisions are located along the Cape May peninsula. The refuge's five-mile stretch along Delaware Bay is a major resting and feeding area for migrating shorebirds and wading birds each spring. It also attracts large numbers of waterfowl, marsh birds, raptors, songbirds, reptiles and amphibians. It includes salt marsh, forested uplands and wetlands, vernal pools, scrub-shrub and grasslands.

The Great Cedar Swamp Division, the largest contiguous forest on the refuge, lies within the Pinelands National Reserve and the Great Egg Harbor National Scenic and Recreational River. It protects hardwood swamp, salt marsh and bog habitats.

Two Mile Beach contains undisturbed beach habitat critical to shorebirds and beach-nesting birds like endangered piping plover and least tern. In addition, this unit protects maritime forest, dune thickets and tidal ponds.

Wildlife to Watch

Shorebirds amass along Delaware Bay beaches from mid-May to mid-June to feast on horseshoe crab eggs, while marsh birds and songbirds begin returning

CAPE MAY-DELAWARE BAY ■ *Cape May National Wildlife Refuge*

to breeding territories. During fall migration American woodcock concentrate in massive numbers in moist woodlands and thickets. They use such habitats for foraging, replenishing their fat reserves by eating more than their weight in earthworms daily. The dawn morning flight for warblers from mid-August through September can be spectacular. Because many raptors choose not to cross large bodies of water like Delaware Bay, many use the bayshore forest edge as a migration corridor. Seventeen raptor species are commonly seen, including peregrine falcon, osprey, northern harrier, American kestrel and Cooper's and sharp-shinned hawks.

Trails

Songbird Trail, a mile-long loop, begins and ends at the refuge office parking area on Kimbles Beach Road. Woodcock Trail has a 1.0-mile-long loop and a 0.75-mile-long spur. Cedar Swamp trail is a 1.0-mile loop. The 1.0-mile Dune Trail traverses the Two Mile Beach Unit through the dune with a 0.1-mile boardwalk spur to a beach overlook. All trails cover easy, level terrain but trail surfaces vary. Trail maps are available online and at the refuge office.

Site Notes The refuge office at Kimbles Beach Road is open Monday through Friday. The Visitor Contact Station at the Two Mile Beach Unit is open sparingly. The beach at Two Mile Beach is closed to public access April 1 to September 30 to protect endangered beachnesting birds but the Dune Trail is open. Site maps are available online. Ticks, chiggers and biting flies are part of the South Jersey fauna.

Size Approximately 8,000 acres

Directions From the Garden State Parkway, take exit 10 west toward Cape May Court House. Go about 0.2 mile and turn left on US 9 south. Go approximately 0.5 mile on US 9 south to Hand Avenue. Turn right and go 3 miles to NJ 47. Turn left. Take a quick right onto Kimbles Beach Road. The refuge office is on the left in about 0.25 mile. Maps and directions to other locations within the CMNWR are available at this office or on the website.

Nearest Town Cape May Court House

Ownership U.S. Fish and Wildlife Service

Contact 609-463-0994; www.fws.gov/northeast/capemay

Features trails, hiking, observation platforms, interpretive signs, checklist, visitor center, drinking water, parking, canoeing/kayaking

Piping Plover   PHOTO BY BOB CUNNINGHAM

Great
▲ SITE ▲

Dennis Creek Wildlife Management Area

PHOTO BY LAURIE PETTIGREW/NJDFW

Description

Dennis Creek Wildlife Management Area encompasses thousands of acres of salt marsh bordering mixed-deciduous forest, pine plantations, Atlantic white cedar drainages and old fields. The jewel in the crown is Jakes Landing. Once the site of the local ship-building industry, the road now bursts from the forest onto the vast, untarnished plain of the salt marsh. The scenic beauty of Jakes Landing is as captivating as its wildlife. Canoeing or kayaking on Dennis Creek is a great way to experience this site.

Wildlife to Watch

Stop frequently along Jakes Landing Road in the spring to look and listen for the spring songbird migrants. Pull off the road and park, then walk or bike along Old Robbins Trail to find ovenbird, wood thrush, black-and-white warbler, Acadian flycatchers, prothonotary warbler and northern flicker. The first half-mile of Jakes Landing passes through open deciduous woods. Listen and look for yellow-throated warbler, rose-breasted grosbeak, Baltimore and orchard oriole, white-eyed vireo and northern parula. The overgrown field on the left is usually good for yellow-breasted chat, blue grosbeak and indigo bunting. As you move into the pine plantation, look for pine warbler and scarlet tanager.

Pay attention as you come to the end of the forest and break out onto the marsh. This transition zone is a particularly good spot to observe songbirds and raptors during migration, especially on spring mornings when fallout occurs. Bald eagles and osprey frequently sit in the dead snags at the edge of the marsh.

Great
▲ SITE ▲

As you enter the marsh, roll your windows down and listen as you drive to the parking area. The marsh reverberates with sound in all seasons. Whether it is the *kek-kek-kek* of rails, the high pitched *wil-wil-willet* and the burble of a marsh wren in summer, the quack of mallards or the thunderous roar of thousands of snow geese in winter, the marsh is never quiet. Clapper, Virginia and black rails breed here in summer, as do northern harrier, eastern meadowlark, seaside and saltmarsh sharp-tailed sparrow, osprey and great horned owl. This is one of the best locations to see short-eared owls in winter and hear whip-poor-wills in summer. Waterfowl include occasional northern pintails, American wigeons, abundant American black ducks, mallards and frequently mergansers. River otter are common but very difficult to see.

Audubon
IMPORTANT
BIRD AREAS

Trails

There are no marked trails at Dennis Creek WMA.

Site Notes Dennis Creek WMA is a natural area with no facilities. It is open for hunting during prescribed seasons. Beware: ticks, chiggers and biting flies are part of the South Jersey fauna.

Size 8,019 acres

Directions From the end of NJ 55, take NJ 47 for approximately 3.0 miles. Bear left onto NJ 347 and continue for approximately 6.0 miles to Jakes Landing Road just north of Dennisville. Turn right and proceed 1.5 miles to the parking lot and boat ramp.

Nearest Town Dennisville

Ownership NJDEP Division of Fish, Game and Wildlife

Contact 856-785-0455; www. njfishandwildlife.com

Features parking, scenic vista, boat launch, canoeing/ kayaking, biking, hiking

Saltmarsh Sharp-tailed Sparrow PHOTO BY BOB CUNNINGHAM

Great
▲ SITE ▲

Dix Wildlife Management Area

PHOTO BY LAURIE PETTIGREW/NJDFW

Description

Dix Wildlife Management Area and Green Swamp Nature Area are bound on the north by the scenic Cohansey River. The Cohansey watershed is largely an agricultural area with fields, nurseries and orchards bordering the river and bay. Dix WMA is a patchwork of old fields and wooded wetlands surrounding Middle Marsh, an extensive area of salt marsh and mudflats. Green Swamp Nature Area provides boat access to the Cohansey River and is a great place to scan for bald eagle and northern harrier. Thousands of snow geese spend the winter in this watershed and can usually be heard if not seen.

Wildlife to Watch

This is the place to see eagles. Scan the trees along the river as you drive down Back Neck Road. Also, check the large fields along the road for sandhill cranes, especially near Green Swamp. Drive to the boat launch area for a spectacular view. Eagles are almost always visible, as are northern harriers. In spring and summer ospreys are common. Walk the large fields by Eagle Manor for sparrows all year. Purple finches are not uncommon in winter. Spring, summer and fall bring a profusion of wood warblers, thrushes, vireos and songbirds. Coyotes are often heard at dusk, and river otter make their presence known with scent piles and otter slides.

Trails

No marked trails exist here but plenty of old roads and unmarked trails go through the woods at Dix. Roads are closed to vehicles from March 15 to

Great
▲ SITE ▲

September 1 and are great for walking and watching. A trail at the end of Middle Marsh Lane leads onto an old dike that is a superb place to scan for bald eagle, river otter, snow geese and other waterfowl in winter. The trail is rough and can be wet or muddy. There is a short, well-marked interpretive trail at Green Swamp Preserve; the trail is easy but not universally accessible.

Site Notes Dix WMA is a natural area with no facilities. Drive slowly as you may encounter many potholes on the gravel roads. Biting fly season can be uncomfortable, especially on hot, still days. Dix WMA is open for hunting during prescribed seasons. Beware: ticks, chiggers and biting flies are part of the South Jersey fauna.

Size Dix WMA: 3,393 acres

Green Swamp: 530 acres

Directions From NJ 55 take exit 29 to CR 552 west. Follow CR 552 west for 6.2 miles to CR 553 south. Turn left onto CR 553 south and travel approximately 5 miles, through the village of Fairton. After turning right at the "T" in the center of Fairton (remaining on CR 53), turn right again in 0.1 mile onto CR 601 (Back Neck Road). Follow CR 601 for 4 miles to Green Swamp entrance on right. Travel 0.5 mile further to Dix WMA. Park at the gate to Eagle Manor and walk the fields or continue 0.1 mile to Schoolhouse Road. Turn left, travel to stop sign and turn right onto Middle Marsh Lane (dirt). Park in the first field on the left and walk either dirt road.

Nearest Town Fairton

Ownership Dix WMA: NJDEP Division of Fish and Wildlife

Green Swamp Nature Preserve: Public Service Enterprise Group

Contact Dix WMA: 856-785-0455; www.njfishandwildlife.com

Green Swamp, managed by The Nature Conservancy: 609-861-0600; www. nature.org/wherewework/

Features trails, hiking, biking, boat launch, boating, parking, scenic view

American Woodcock PHOTO BY STEVE BYLAND

Great
▲ SITE ▲

Raybins Beach

PHOTO COURTESY OF WWW.HOGANPHOTO.COM

Description

The landscape of the Glades is striking and diverse, encompassing tidal marsh, mature oak-pine woodlands, old-growth swamp forests, early successional woodlands and beachfront along the Delaware Bay. The Glades was once part of the area's agricultural and maritime economy and includes crumbling farm-building foundations and fields reverting to woodland.

Egg Island Wildlife Management Area is a vast, windswept salt marsh, dotted with hummocks of cedar trees, bayberry bushes, sumac and common reeds. A large pond in the middle of the tract attracts wintering waterfowl. The best way to experience Egg Island WMA is by boat, but there are access points at the ends of Turkey Point and Hansey Creek Roads.

Wildlife to Watch

The tidal marshes along Maple Avenue and Turkey Point Road are excellent places to spot bald eagles. Golden eagle and rough-legged hawk are possible too. Scan the marsh at Turkey Point or Hansey Creek for northern harrier, red-tailed hawk, short-eared owl, great horned owl and very rarely, snowy owl. Walk along Hansey Creek Road to look for butterfly species like Henry's elfin, holly azure, blueberry azure, Aaron's skipper and salt marsh skipper. Thousands of snow geese feed and rest in the marsh, and common and hooded merganser, ruddy duck, bufflehead, mallard, northern pintail, American black duck and green-winged teal can usually be seen. You may see breeding songbirds like common yellowthroat, yellow warbler, gray catbird and northern mockingbird. Raybins

Beach at the south end of Fortescue is one of the best spots on the bay for watching the spring arrival of shorebirds and horseshoe crabs.

Audubon
IMPORTANT
BIRD AREAS

Trails

There are three short trails: the Warfle Farm Trail, Bald Eagle Trail and Maple Street Trail. Trail guides are available at www.natlands.org/preserves/preserve.asp?fldPreserveId=39.

Site Notes The Glades allows limited hunting during deer seasons by permit only.

Egg Island WMA is a natural area with no facilities. It is open for hunting during prescribed seasons. Remember: ticks, chiggers and biting flies are part of the South Jersey fauna.

Size The Glades: 7,500 acres

Egg Island WMA: 6,714 acres

Directions From the end of NJ 55, take NJ 47 south for 3.2 miles to the traffic light. Turn right onto CR 670 toward Mauricetown. Travel 2.2 miles to Highland Street (2nd blinking light). Turn right and proceed 5.3 miles (Highland Street becomes CR 676) to a "T" that intersects with County Route 553. Turn right onto CR 553 and proceed 0.2 mile to Maple Avenue on your left. Drive along Maple Avenue and cross over the causeway. Park on the western side and walk back to scan for wildlife. Continue straight for another 2.0 miles to the end of the road. To reach Hansey Creek Road turn left at the intersection of CR 676 and CR 553. Travel 0.25 mile to Hansey Creek Road on the right.

Nearest Town Fortescue

Ownership The Glades: Natural Lands Trust

Egg Island WMA: NJDEP Division of Fish, Game and Wildlife

Contact The Glades: 856-825-9952; www.natlands.org

Egg Island WMA: 856-785-0455; www.njfishandwildlife.com

Features parking, trails, hiking, observation tower, boat launch

Blackburnian Warbler PHOTO BY BOB CUNNINGHAM

Great
▲ SITE ▲

East Point Lighthouse

PHOTO BY LAURIE PETTIGREW/NJDFW

Description

Heislerville WMA is on the Delaware Bay, the premier resting and feeding stop for hundreds of thousands of shorebirds during spring migration. Strategically located midway between wintering grounds of South America and the nesting grounds of the Arctic, the marsh's value for waterfowl cannot be underestimated.

Wildlife to Watch

See waterfowl, wading birds and shorebirds from the impoundments at Matts Landing. Check the open water near the spillways in winter to see foraging divers such as common and hooded merganser, ruddy duck and grebes. See wading birds from the dirt road atop the dikes. Work the shrubs along the road for warblers and songbirds. Scan the cedar hummocks for snowy egrets and black-crowned night herons. In spring, the mudflats attract thousands of red knots, ruddy turnstones, dunlin and sandpipers.

East Point Light, the most photographed lighthouse in New Jersey, was built in 1849. Here, the fall migration of butterflies and dragonflies is spectacular. Scan the marsh for northern harriers, peregrine falcons and rough-legged hawks. In spring, warblers, thrushes, flickers and sparrows feed and rest in the shrubs, and shorebirds feast on protein-rich horseshoe-crab eggs on the beach. Diamondback terrapin come ashore in June to lay their eggs, and this is one of the best bayshore spots to see the fall hawk migration.

Share the observation platform on Thompson's Beach Road with a variety of gulls and terns to see the vast restored tidal marsh. Look for northern harrier, peregrine falcon, osprey, herons, egrets, clapper rail, black and turkey vultures, bald eagles and American black ducks. Thousands of snow geese winter on this marsh, and the din they raise when agitated is breathtaking. Walk the road to Thompson's Beach to view rafts of wintering waterfowl or great concentrations of shorebirds in the spring. In summer look for egrets, glossy ibis, nesting seaside sparrows and willets.

Audubon
IMPORTANT
BIRD AREAS

Trails

The only marked trails are at Matts Landing, where a 0.25-mile interpretive trail contains an observation platform and a photo blind. A 1-mile paved bike path connects Matts Landing to Cumberland County's bike trail system.

Site Notes Heislerville WMA is open for hunting during prescribed seasons.

Size Heislerville: 6,739 acres

Thompson's Beach: 1,400 acres

Directions Matts Landing: From NJ 55 and NJ 47, travel 5.3 miles on NJ 47 south to Mackey's Lane. Turn right onto Mackey's Lane and go 0.3 mile to CR 616 (Dorchester-Heislerville Road). Turn left and travel 2.2 miles to Matts Landing Road. Turn right and proceed 0.5 mile. The impoundments will be on either side.

East Point: Turn left at the end of Matts Landing Road and proceed past the marinas to the dirt road on your left. Take this along the top of the impoundments to follow the 8-mile auto-trail. The dirt road ends at East Point Road. Or, follow Matts Landing Road back to CR 616 (Main Street). Turn right on CR 616 and right again on East Point Road to Lighthouse Lane.

Thompson's Beach: Take East Point Road back into Heislerville. Continue straight as East Point Road becomes Glade Road at its junction with CR 616. Turn right onto Thompson's Beach Road and follow to the small parking area at the end of the paved road.

Nearest Town Heislerville

Ownership Heislerville WMA: NJDEP Division of Fish, Game and Wildlife

Thompson's Beach: Public Service Enterprise Group

Contact Heislerville WMA: 609-785-0455; www.njfishandwildlife.com

Thompson's Beach: 1-888-MARSHES; www.pseg.com/environment2008/estuary/overview.jsp, managed by The Nature Conservancy: 609-861-0600; www.nature.org/newjersey

Features parking, hiking, observation platform, boat launch, restrooms, photo blind, interpretive signs

Great
▲ SITE ▲

View from Stone Harbor Viewing Platform

PHOTO BY LILLIAN ARMSTRONG/NJAS

Description

Located at the southern end of Seven Mile Island, Stone Harbor Point (SHP) encompasses several acres of dense undergrowth at its northern end and vast acres of sand flats, low sand dunes and salt marshes. The typography of the sandy southern end of SHP is in constant flux, a result of tides, ocean storms, prevailing winds and ocean currents. During a spring full-moon tide, the southern end of SHP is often completely awash, with only a few of the dunes remaining above water.

In some years Champagne Island (located in the middle of Hereford Inlet) is almost completely submerged. When visible, it is used by colonial beach nesters. The tidal beach, marshlands and low grassy dune habitat make SHP a critical site for migrating birds and threatened and endangered beach nesters.

Wildlife to Watch

Virtually every shorebird seen in Cape May County can be found here. These include sanderling, semipalmated, least and western sandpipers, black-bellied plover and dunlin, red knot and eastern willet. Popular beach-nesting species include piping plover, American oystercatcher, black skimmers and common and least tern. The marshes at Stone Harbor Point are home to great blue, little blue and tricolored herons, as well as snowy and great egrets. In recent years a sizeable colony of royal terns has nested on Champagne Island. Offshore, from fall to spring, surf, black and common scoter, northern gannet and common and red-throated loons may be seen. Long-tailed ducks, brant and bufflehead congregate in the calmer waters of the inlet. In winter months purple sandpipers often occupy the rocky oceanside jetty. A variety of sparrows and other passerines nest just south of the parking lot. Fall brings concentrations of songbirds. Monarch butterflies congregate here on September evenings on their way south. Recent winters have brought snowy owls and snow buntings. Other birds of prey, especially peregrine falcons, patrol the area for prey year-round.

Stone Harbor Point is also a nesting area for diamondback terrapins. Horseshoe crabs and hermit crabs are plentiful. Shell collectors frequent the beaches; keep an eye out for jellyfish on the beach in the summer.

Trails

Interpretive signs from the parking area to other locations were installed in 2009 and guide visitors to viewing platforms and educational signage.

Site Notes	During the breeding season, from early spring until Labor Day, a large part of SHP is fenced off to protect breeding shorebirds, especially piping plovers. Dogs are not allowed on SHP or on Champagne Island.
Size	350 acres
Directions	From the Garden State Parkway, turn east at exit 10 onto Stone Harbor Boulevard. (This is one of the few exits near the end of the GSP that has a traffic signal.) Follow Stone Harbor Boulevard into town. Proceed through town to First Avenue. Turn right and take First Avenue to its end at a large parking area.
Nearest Town	Stone Harbor
Ownership	Borough of Stone Harbor
Contact	609-368-5102; www.stone-harbor.nj.us
Features	parking, observation platform, scenic views

Spring Waders on Nummy Island

PHOTO BY BOB CUNNINGHAM

Great
▲ SITE ▲

Villas Wildlife Management Area

PHOTO BY LAURIE PETTIGREW/NJDFW

Description

Villas WMA was, until recently, a golf course and resort. Surrounded by residential development, it is just north of the Cape May Canal and two blocks east of Delaware Bay. Now managed primarily for migratory birds, it is a birder's paradise. This 253-acre site contains a mosaic of habitats, including open woodland, wooded wetland, small pools with emergent vegetation, an eight-acre pond, tidal marsh, grassland and meadow. Plans call for the reforestation of some areas and the creation of scrub-shrub habitat and vernal pools in others. Villas WMA falls within the lower 10 kilometers of the Cape May Peninsula, long recognized by biologists as being one of the most significant natural areas in the state. It faces tremendous development pressure. Undeveloped areas such as this serve as critical stopover sites for major concentrations of migrants, particularly in the fall, when birds fly south along the coast to Delaware Bay. Birds will stop to rest and feed before crossing the bay with favorable winds.

Wildlife to Watch

This is a great place to see songbirds, woodpeckers and raptors. The best times to bird watch here are May and October, but wildlife can be seen any time of year. Spring migration brings eastern phoebe, eastern kingbird, white-eyed vireo, purple martin, tree swallow, northern parula, yellow, black-and-white and prairie warbler, common yellowthroat, indigo bunting and the occasional bobolink. You'll see American goldfinch here year-round, as well as red-winged blackbird, northern cardinal, gray catbird, field sparrow, Carolina wren, northern mockingbird and American robin. Fall is most interesting with the arrival of raptors.

Great
▲ SITE ▲

Migrants include broad-winged, red-shouldered, sharp-shinned and Cooper's hawks, American kestrel, peregrine falcon, merlin and turkey and black vultures. Warbler transients include Tennessee, orange-crowned, yellow-rumped and palm warblers. Listen and look for most of the common woodpeckers: downy, hairy, red-bellied, northern flicker and yellow-bellied sapsucker. Check the pond and small pools for waterfowl, sandpipers, wading birds, frogs and turtles.

Trails

There are more than five miles of trails winding through the site. Most of the trails are paved, flat and fairly accessible to everyone. The longest trail, leading along the edge of Cox Hall Creek and through wooded wetlands, is an old gravel road.

Site Notes	This site is a natural area with no facilities.
Size	253 acres
Directions	From the end of the Garden State Parkway, take NJ 109 north for 0.5 mile to US 9 south. Stay on US 9 south for approximately 1.5 miles to Bayshore Road. Turn right onto Bayshore Road (CR 603). Go approximately 2.4 miles to Shawmount Avenue. Turn left and travel to the gravel parking area.
Nearest Town	Villas
Ownership	NJDEP Division of Fish and Wildlife
Contact	856-785-0455; www.njfishandwildlife.com
Features	hiking, trails, biking, parking

Black-and-white Warbler

PHOTO BY BOB CUNNINGHAM

Great
▲ SITE ▲

Description

Situated on the southern edge of the Pine Barrens, Eldora Nature Preserve is the first preserve established by The Nature Conservancy expressly for the protection of rare moths. Habitats include mixed-hardwood swamps, vernal wetlands, salt marshes, fields, an old orchard and pine-oak woodlands.

Wildlife to Watch

Eldora's mosaic of habitats supports a variety of moths, butterflies and skippers, including three species of azures, Henry's elfin and falcate orangetip. The butterfly garden complements the natural communities while offering the most reliable viewing of rare skipper—a globally rare species. Barred owls winter at the preserve, and migrating songbirds and hawks congregate in the woods during spring and fall. Don't forget that ticks, chiggers and biting flies are part of the South Jersey fauna.

Trails

A 3.25-mile loop trail system covers easy to moderate terrain on varied surfaces. The main trail quickly opens up to a boardwalk with a raised wildlife observation platform that provides a panoramic view of the salt marsh, forest edge and West Creek. The trail is well maintained but not universally accessible.

Site Notes: Eldora Preserve is open daily from dawn to dusk. No pets please. The visitor center is open Monday through Thursday.

Size: 201 acres

Directions: From the end of NJ 55, continue south onto NJ 47. At the fork for NJ 47 and NJ 347, continue straight on NJ 47, past the gas station and Wawa. Continue for 7.6 miles to Eldora Preserve on the left.

Nearest Town: Eldora

Ownership: The Nature Conservancy

Contact: 609-861-0600; www.nature.org/newjersey

Features: restrooms, parking, trails, observation platform, visitor center, picnicking

Millville Wildlife Management Area 97

Description

The Millville Wildlife Management Area is characterized by extensive oak-pine forest interspersed with freshwater wetlands, sandwash ponds and early successional habitats, including scrub-shrub and grasslands. These early successional habitats support breeding red-headed woodpecker and a number of scrub-shrub dependant birds, including prairie warbler, blue-winged warbler and American woodcock. The mixture and expansive size of the habitats at Millville ensure its place as a significant stopover site for spring and fall migrants and as a nesting site for interior forest nesters and early-successional specialists.

CAPE MAY-DELAWARE BAY ■ Other Sites

Other sites

Wildlife to Watch

Walk the forest roads and listen and look for scarlet tanager, tufted titmouse, black-and-white warbler, broad-winged hawk, wild turkey, wood thrush, Acadian flycatcher and worm-eating warbler. A trip along the edges of fields should reveal gray catbird, brown thrasher, northern flicker, Baltimore oriole, blue grosbeak, indigo bunting, field sparrow, prairie warbler and eastern kingbird. White-tailed deer come out to feed at dusk, and gray squirrel scold from their perch in a tree. Look for fence lizards basking in the sun on fallen logs. Scan the old sandwash ponds for waterfowl, osprey and bald eagle.

Audubon
IMPORTANT
BIRD AREAS

Trails

There are no marked trails at this site, but many miles of dirt and abandoned roads and firebreaks provide hours of hiking and biking opportunities. This is an expansive site and a map is useful. Site maps are available online.

Site Notes: Millville WMA is a natural area with no facilities and is open for hunting during prescribed seasons. Remember: ticks, chiggers and biting flies are part of the South Jersey fauna.

Size: 15,672 acres

Directions: From the end of NJ 55, take NJ 47 south for 3.2 miles to the traffic light. Turn right onto CR 670 toward Mauricetown and go 1 mile to blinker light after bridge. Turn right, staying on CR 670 for 1.5 miles to CR 718 (Ackley Road). Turn left onto Ackley Road and travel 1 mile to stop sign at Spring Garden Road. Start birding anywhere along Ackley Road after crossing Spring Garden.

Nearest Town: Millville

Ownership: NJDEP Division of Fish and Wildlife

Contact: 856-785-0455; www.njfishandwildlife.com

Features: parking, hiking, biking

NJAS, Cape May Bird Observatory   98

Description

The grounds at the CMBO Center in Goshen were planted to attract wildlife, especially butterflies in late summer. Over thirty species of butterflies have been counted on a single day in this relatively small plot. The center is also home to a wide variety of educational programs and workshops throughout the year.

Wildlife to Watch

The bird feeder station is alive with birds and can provide an outdoor classroom for species identification. You may find five species of sparrow at a time, in addition to Carolina wren, brown thrasher and northern cardinal. Snakes are also common, including black rat, garter and green snakes. Come summer, be on the lookout for caterpillars, butterflies and moths. Buckeyes, black swallowtails, clouded and cloudless sulphers and the occasional rare long-tailed skipper may be seen.

Trails

A short trail runs through the gardens and around the circumference of the fields.

Site Notes: Be sure to check the NJAS website www.birdcapemay.org for information on hours of operation, upcoming programs, schedule of weekly walks, wildlife checklists, maps and local businesses.

Size: 27 acres

Directions: From the end of southbound NJ 55, continue south onto NJ 47. At the fork for NJ 47 and NJ 347, bear left onto NJ 347, which will rejoin NJ 47 just north of Dennisville, and continue south for several miles. Go straight through the traffic light at CR 657 and continue exactly 1 mile. The center will be on your left just around a bend in the road.

Nearest Town: Cape May Court House

Ownership: New Jersey Audubon Society

Contact: 609-861-0700; www.njaudubon.org, www.birdcapemay.org

Features: visitor center, observation deck, trail, checklist, restrooms, drinking water, interpretive programs

Peaslee Wildlife Management Area   99

Description

One of the largest wildlife management areas in the state, Peaslee has thousands of acres of upland pine-oak forests and lowland bogs. Its longest border is the upper part of the Tuckahoe River. Old cranberry bogs and a mill pond are succeeding to wet meadow and offer excellent freshwater habitats.

Wildlife to Watch

Peaslee is at its best in spring and early summer. Look for Allegheny mound ant mounds along Cumberland and First Avenues. Listen and look for most woodland wildlife, including wild turkeys, prairie warblers, northern cardinal, eastern towhee, red-headed, red-bellied, hairy and downy woodpecker, tufted titmouse, American crow, indigo bunting, chipping sparrow, pine warbler, yellow-billed cuckoo, great-crested flycatcher and bobwhite quail. White-tailed deer come out at dusk to feed in the fields.

Trails

There are no marked trails at Peaslee, but miles of dirt roads and old, abandoned roads are great for hiking or mountain biking. Site maps are available online.

Site Notes: This is a natural area with no facilities. Peaslee is open for hunting during prescribed seasons. Remember: ticks, chiggers and biting flies are part of the South Jersey fauna.

Size: 19,923 acres

Other sites

Directions: From New Jersey 55 exit 24, take New Jersey 49 east to Hesstown Road, about 5 miles. Turn left and proceed 1.7 miles to the sand road on your left. Turn left on the sand road for a 1.6-mile auto tour loop. You will exit at Hesstown Road. To get to Bennetts Mill, return on Hesstown Road to NJ 49. Turn right (west) and travel 1.2 miles to County Route 671 (Union Road). Turn right and travel 4 miles to Old Mays Landing Road (first right turn). Turn right and travel less than 1 mile to bridge. Mill pond is on your left.

Nearest Town: Millville

Ownership: NJDEP Division of Fish, Game and Wildlife

Contact: 856-785-0455; www.njfishandwildlife.com

Features: parking, interpretive signs

PSEG Bayside Restoration Site   100

Description

This extensive coastal wetland tract, one of PSEG's Estuary Enhancement sites, contains thousands of acres of salt marsh bisected by miles of tidal creeks. A narrow border of upland was preserved to help maintain water quality, protect the natural and cultural resources of this rural, agrarian community and to provide public access.

Wildlife to Watch

This site is good for waterfowl, shorebirds, songbirds and hawks. Ring-billed gulls flock to the fields during cultivation. Marsh wrens, clapper rail and willets call throughout the nesting season. Seeing bald eagles is almost guaranteed. Look for short-eared owl and northern harrier on Ragged Island Road in winter.

Trails

There are no trails at this site but visitors can walk the roads and field edges.

Site Notes: Information about the Estuary Enhancement Program and site maps are available at www.pseg.com/environment2008/estuary/pdf/map-CRW.pdf. Bayside is open daily from dawn to dusk. Hunting is permitted during prescribed seasons. Remember: ticks, chiggers and biting flies are part of the South Jersey fauna.

Size: 4,384 acres

Directions: From the junction of NJ 49 and NJ 77 in Bridgeton, proceed 1.7 miles west on NJ 49 to left turn onto West Avenue. Proceed 0.2 mile and turn right on CR 607. Go 6.9 miles to the center of Greenwich. Turn right on CR 623 (Ye Greate Street), then left on CR 642 (Bacon's Neck Road). Go 1.7 miles to a "T" intersection and turn right onto Tyndall Island Road. Go 0.3 mile and turn left onto Bayside Road. Make another left onto Caviar Tower Road. Or, turn left on Tydall Island Road and follow it or Ragged Island Road to their ends.

Nearest Town: Greenwich

Ownership: Public Service Enterprise Group (PSEG)

Contact: 888-MARSHES

Features: parking

CAPE MAY-DELAWARE BAY ■ Other Sites

Other sites

239

Reeds Beach

101

Description

The northern end of the small, private community of Reeds Beach has remnant sand dunes and coastal vegetation. Horseshoe crabs come ashore to lay their protein-rich eggs in May and June. Peak migration usually occurs around the full moon in May. Millions of the crabs' small green eggs are laid in the sand and become food for birds. In fact, Reeds Beach is the site where this phenomenon was first discovered in the 1980s, and it is the most consistent site from which to observe this process. For migrating shorebirds this stop is essential to provide the food they need to continue on to their Arctic nesting grounds.

Wildlife to Watch

In May an observation platform is erected on the beach for shorebird viewing. Thousands of shorebirds and gulls feast on the crab eggs including laughing gulls, ruddy turnstones, semi-palmated sandpipers, sanderlings, red knots, dunlin and least sandpipers.

Site Notes: Park at Smoky's Marina at the end of Reeds Beach Road. A donation of $1.00 is requested.

Size: 12' x 12' platform

Directions: Reeds Beach Road is slightly more than 2 miles north of Norburys Landing Road on NJ 47. Turn left and travel 1 mile into town. Turn right onto Beach Avenue and continue to parking lot at the end of the road.

Nearest Town: Reeds Beach

Ownership: Multiple owners

Contact: 609-628-2436: NJDEP Endangered and Nongame Species Program

Features: parking, observation platform

Stow Creek State Park

102

Description

Bald eagles are making a comeback in southern New Jersey, and this site provides a terrific opportunity to see an eagle. The large sycamore standing next to an abandoned farmhouse at the edge of Stow Creek was the location of one of New Jersey's first eagle nests following the Division of Fish and Wildlife's restoration efforts in the 1980s and 90s. This site still provides plenty of opportunities to see bald eagles, nesting osprey and a variety of wading birds and marsh wildlife species.

Wildlife to Watch

In New Jersey nesting bald eagles reside year-round, usually remaining in the area of their nest. Many juveniles and adults spend the winter in the Delaware Bayshore region where open water and abundant food provide good conditions.

Look for wrens and swallows that feed on the plentiful insects. When the eagles are away or quiet, watch the marsh for rails, wetland songbirds, muskrats, crabs and fish. Look also for nesting osprey, snowy egret, green and great blue heron, Canada geese and mallards.

Trails

There are currently no trails at this site.

Site Notes: Stow Creek Park is a natural area with no facilities. Remember: ticks, chiggers and biting flies are part of the South Jersey fauna.

Size: About 1,200 acres

Directions: From the junction of New Jersey 49 and NJ 45 in Salem, travel 0.7 mile east on NJ 49 for 2.5 miles to CR 650 (Quinton-Hancocks Road). Turn right onto CR 650 and go 1.5 miles to CR 623 (New Bridge Road). Go approximately 6 miles to the parking area on the right side of the road just after crossing the bridge over Stow Creek.

Nearest Town: Canton, Lower Alloways Creek Township

Ownership: NJDEP Division of Parks and Forests

Contact: 856-935-3218; www.njparksandforests.org

Features: parking, barrier-free

Tuckahoe Wildlife Management Area   103

Description

The scenic Tuckahoe River winds its way to the Great Egg Harbor River and Bay through an expanse of salt marsh and tidal creeks which is excellent for bird watching. Six brackish water impoundments on the upland edges of the tract also provide good bird watching opportunities. Located on the edge of the Pine Barrens, the woodlands bordering the salt marsh are a mixture of pine and oak trees. A hardwood swamp and small freshwater lake provide additional habitat for beaver, turtles, frogs and fish.

Wildlife to Watch

Drive the dirt roads through the various habitats on the WMA or park and walk to see chipping sparrows, American goldfinches, pine warblers, indigo buntings, yellow-billed cuckoos, prothonotary warblers, common yellow-throats, marsh wrens, Carolina wrens and northern flickers in the scrub-shrub, woodlands and small fields along the roads. Scan the marsh and impoundments for waders, gulls, shorebirds and waterfowl. Tuckahoe is a reliable location for wintering tundra swans and golden eagle during fall migration.

Audubon
IMPORTANT
BIRD AREAS

Trails

There are no marked trails at Tuckahoe, but there are miles of dirt roads, dikes and old, abandoned roads suitable for hiking or mountain biking. Site maps are available online.

Site Notes: Tuckahoe is a natural area with few facilities. It is open for hunting during prescribed seasons. Remember: ticks, chiggers and biting flies are part of the South Jersey fauna.

Size: 14,724 acres

Directions: From the junction of US 9 and NJ 50 in Seaville, take NJ 50 north for 4.8 miles to CR 631. Turn right and travel 0.3 mile to WMA entrance on the left. The office is in 0.5 mile. Continue straight for 1 mile to boat launch. To go to Corbin City, continue north on NJ 50 for 3 miles to Griscom Mill Road. Turn right. The road turns to sand and gravel and continues for 8 miles past the impoundments before it intersects again with NJ 50 as Gibson Creek Road.

Nearest Town: Tuckahoe

Ownership: NJDEP Division of Fish, Game and Wildlife

Contact: 856-785-0455; www.njfishandwildlife.com

Features: parking, boat ramp, canoeing/kayaking, hiking, mountain biking, observation platform

Wetlands Institute · 104

Description

There are 6,000 acres of salt marsh visible from this uniquely designed education center. From its glass-enclosed great room to its many levels of decks and a three-story tall observation tower, this center begs visitors to look outside. The delightful education center with hands-on exhibits brings the outdoors in, and Marion's Garden features hundreds of native plants chosen to attract birds and butterflies. Guided boat tours and kayak trips are offered in summer, and family-oriented educational programs are offered year-round.

Wildlife to Watch

Salt marsh critters are what you will find here. Northern diamondback terrapins are the focus of the Terrapin Conservation Project, one of many Institute research projects. An "osprey cam" reveals the raising of osprey chicks. This site abounds with gulls, terns, shorebirds, waders and waterfowl.

Trails

Enjoy the 0.25-mile audio-guided nature trail.

Site Notes: The Wetlands Institute is open Monday through Saturday from 9:30 a.m. to 4:30 p.m. and Sunday 10 a.m. to 4:30 p.m. from May 15 to October 15. The Institute is closed Sunday and Monday the rest of the year. Call to verify hours.

Size: 34 acres

Directions: Take exit 10B from the Garden State Parkway east toward Stone Harbor. The institute is 2.9 miles on the right side of the road.

Nearest Town: Stone Harbor

Ownership: Private non-profit

Contact: 609-368-1211; www.wetlandsinstitute.org

Features: interpretive center, interpretive programs, gift shop, observation platform, scenic overlook, interpretive signage, restrooms, drinking water, kayaking

Ruby-throated Hummingbird

Red-eyed Vireo

Other sites

Index